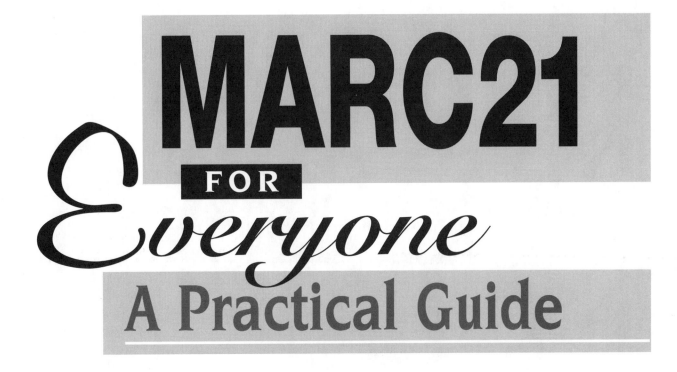

MARC21
FOR
Everyone
A Practical Guide

DEBORAH A. FRITZ
RICHARD J. FRITZ

AMERICAN LIBRARY
ASSOCIATION
Chicago
2003

While extensive effort has gone into ensuring the reliability of information appearing in this book, the publisher makes no warranty, express or implied, on the accuracy or reliability of the information, and does not assume and hereby disclaims any liability to any person for any loss or damage caused by errors or omissions in this publication.

The OCLC materials herein are used with OCLC's permission, and copyrights in the material belong to OCLC Online Computer Library Center, Inc.

Library of Congress Cataloging-in-Publication Data

Fritz, Deborah A. (Deborah Angela), 1955–
    MARC21 for everyone : a practical guide / by Deborah A. Fritz and Richard J. Fritz.
        p.   cm.
    Includes bibliographical references and index.
    ISBN 0-8389-0842-X (alk. paper)
    1. MARC formats—Handbooks, manuals, etc. 2. MARC formats—Problems, exercises, etc. I. Title: MARC21 for everyone. II. Fritz, Richard J., 1950– III. Title.
    Z699.35.M28 F75 2003
    025.3′16—dc21   2002014138

Printed in the United States of America

07 06 05   5 4 3 2

CONTENTS

ILLUSTRATIONS

TABLES

PREFACE

This book grew out of many years of giving a workshop called, so enticingly, "Introduction to MARC." As the handout for the workshop expanded to book length, it began to seem increasingly feasible that it could become the MARC book that our publisher said the library world still needed.

Eventually we broke under the pressure and wrote this book for anyone who wants to know a little bit about MARC and how it works in a library catalog. We like to think that it will be useful to anyone involved with libraries—from a library trustee to someone just getting started in cataloging. For many people, the brief treatment of MARC given here will be more than sufficient. For others, this book will only begin to whet their appetites, but that is by design. For the latter—such as catalogers and systems staff—who require much more in-depth information in this area, the resources are already available. And for those who do not really want to know too much about this thing called MARC in the first place, we are trying to provide a painless and, we hope, successful encounter.

Some very good introductions to MARC are already available. Our favorite is Walt Crawford's *MARC for Library Use*. This is the book we have always gone to when we have difficult questions about MARC not answered by the coding manuals. On a much less intense level is the booklet "Understanding MARC," originally created by the Follett Software Company and now available on the LC MARC home page. This publication offers a quick and readable introduction to MARC.

Our approach to this topic differs from that of others in three major areas. First, we believe that anything that simply lists and explains MARC tags, subfields, indicators, and codes—even with examples—is quickly going to prove overwhelming for any reader who is not a cataloger. Second, we believe that, in a library environment, MARC should never be discussed outside the context of the cataloging rules (AACR2). Finally, because MARC is simply a coding scheme for entering bibliographic information into computer records, we believe that an introduction to MARC should spend some time explaining how these records work in the library online catalog.

Let us make it clear at the outset that this book is by no means a comprehensive treatment of MARC, cataloging, or library automation systems. On the contrary, it is highly selective and includes only what we thought might be interesting at a beginner's level. *Please do not use this book to do cataloging!* In our discussion of MARC coding, we focus on a narrow selection of MARC fields that we think might provide the nontechnical user with an insight into how this whole MARC business works. We intentionally omit any discussion of the most difficult areas of MARC coding.

We have tried to make a dry, technical subject readable and as interesting as possible. This is a difficult task, as we have discovered.

Deborah and Richard Fritz
http://www.marcofquality.com

INTRODUCTION

Everything should be made as simple as possible, but not simpler.

—ALBERT EINSTEIN

This book is intended for those who, for whatever reason, feel they need to know a little bit about MARC. More importantly, this book has been written for those who really don't care about MARC, don't think it is important, can't see why they should have to know anything about it, really don't *want* to know anything about it, but still, after all is said and done, realize that they do need to know *something* about it.

Perhaps we should have been able to make this whole MARC thing incredibly simple and easy to understand, but we couldn't because it isn't simple and easy to understand. You will not learn everything there is to know about MARC from this book, but what you will (we hope) get from it is a good *idea* of how MARC works and a solid grasp of why MARC is important.

What is MARC? MARC is a lot of things, but for the purpose of this book, MARC is defined as a standard for entering bibliographic information into a computer record that can be used by a library automation system to provide a library catalog.

Included in this bibliographic information and, therefore, in MARC records are:

descriptions of library materials;

searchable headings, such as authors and subjects; and

elements to organize collections, such as classification numbers.

There are a few different approaches to the question What is MARC? One approach is for you to go to an "introductory" workshop where someone talks about tags, subfields, and coding for a number of hours. You may need to attend such a workshop at some stage, to learn more about the intricacies of MARC coding. But as a starting point, we think that you will understand more and remember more if you know the *reasons* underlying MARC and how MARC is meant to work in a library's automated system. Whether or not you are a cataloger, we feel that if you know how MARC affects patrons, then perhaps you will find MARC as fascinating as we do.

Who needs to know MARC? We believe that everyone who works in a library should know something about MARC, but especially library directors, reference librarians, acquisitions and circulation people, and, obviously, systems people and catalogers and their support staff! See chapter 6 for more particulars on who needs to know what.

Why do you need to know MARC? Because we now use library automation systems instead of catalog cards in most libraries (or, if we still use catalog cards, we may not for much longer), and because the database at the core of most library automation systems is made up of records in this MARC format, you should know how MARC functions.

If you know how your MARC records are supposed to work, you will discover two rather important things about your automated catalog:

1. Why patrons can find some items in your catalog and not find others.
2. Why patrons can see certain information in your catalog and not see other information.

You will be glad to know more about MARC if you have ever asked such questions as these:

Why can I find a book by its author but not its title?

Why does the catalog say I have six Spanish books when I know I have hundreds?

Why can't I find *Hamlet* the video without wading through every book record in the catalog to get to it?

What happened to the record for such-and-such book? It was there yesterday—but now I can't find it anywhere.

How can you learn MARC? Take it step by step. Perhaps you began the process at library school, perhaps you have had some on-the-job training, or maybe you are starting from scratch here and now. This book will take you the first few steps on your way.

By the way, we are going to use the terms *MARC* and *MARC21* interchangeably throughout this book. We'll explain the history of these terms in a later chapter, but for now, you just need to know that MARC21 is simply the most current version of MARC used in most English-speaking countries.

MARC21 for Everyone is organized in such a way that you should be able to read a bit, do a quick quiz, take a break, read a bit more, and so on, eventually working your way through the book with a minimum of pain and stress.

MARC21 for Everyone is copiously illustrated with examples that will, we hope, clarify some of the many cataloging terms that the experts love to throw around.

Topics

Here is a general outline of what we are going to cover in the pages to follow.

Part I: MARC: The Underlying Fundamentals

Chapter 1: Library Patrons, Bibliographic Information, and the Library Catalog

We begin by introducing the educational, informational, and recreational needs of patrons. We then examine how we provide bibliographic information in library catalogs to make library materials accessible to patrons to meet those needs. There is a brief, introductory mention of how MARC fits into this picture.

Chapter 2: The Rules for Bibliographic Information and the Standards for MARC

Next, we discuss why libraries follow rules when they are supplying bibliographic information for patrons, and how following these rules makes it easier for patrons to find out about our materials and decide whether those materials truly satisfy their needs. We also take a quick look at how those rules connect to MARC.

Chapter 3: MARC21 Records: What Are They, Why Do We Need Them, and How Do We Get Them?

Here we consider what MARC is, how it got started, and how it continues to develop. We also touch on the different kinds of MARC available, why we need the MARC standards, and how we get MARC records.

Chapter 4: MARC21 and the Computerized Catalogs of Today

We move on to consider how MARC is used in the catalogs of today, beginning with how patrons search in our catalogs and how the results of those searches are displayed. Even though displays vary among different catalogs, we will see that all displays come from the same MARC records.

Chapter 5: MARC21 Terminology

It might help you to know that when we talk about MARC records, we use many of the same terms we used when we typed catalog cards. We will describe what some of those older terms mean, then look at some new MARC terms.

Chapter 6: MARC21—Who Needs to Know What

Before we move on to some actual MARC coding, we briefly describe the MARC codes that might be of particular interest to people in various departments of the library.

Part II: MARC21 Codes You Should Know

This section will introduce you to actual coding in specific fields that you will commonly encounter in MARC records. It is the longest section in the book and explains how to code actual fields, indicators, subfields, and so on.

Chapter 7: Indexed Fields—Headings

Indexed fields contain names, titles, and subjects that patrons might use to search for the materials in our collections. There are definite patterns in the

MARC coding for these headings fields that you may find surprisingly easy to remember.

Chapter 8: Display Fields—Bibliographic Description

Display fields contain the descriptions of the materials in our collections that we want to show patrons. All these fields are meant to be displayed to patrons. Some of them are also searchable in both browse and keyword indexes, some are searchable only in keyword indexes, and some are for informational purposes only and are not indexed at all.

Chapter 9: Coded Fields

Coded fields contain important codes that are used by library automation systems. They are never displayed to patrons.

Chapter 10: Number Fields

Number fields contain important numbers that are used by catalogers, systems staff, library automation systems, and sometimes patrons. Some number fields are indexed, and some are displayed to patrons; we concentrate on the ones that are used for finding matching records.

Chapter 11: Summary

We attempt to summarize and distill the contents of the entire book into two pages!

Chapter 12: MARC21 Sample Records

Most of the chapters in this book end with a simple quiz, and we also wrap things up with a final look at some sample records so that you can practice reading them.

Conventions

In this book:

# indicates a blank space

words in bold type are defined in the glossary at the end of the book

## PART I

MARC: The Underlying Fundamentals

1

Library Patrons, Bibliographic Information, and the Library Catalog

Figure 1-1 shows what we are eventually going to get around to talking about—a **MARC record,** a marvelous invention, simply *packed* with information for people and automated systems. Before we can explore the details of this superbly designed **record,** however, we have to take a step back, look at the bigger picture, and see how **MARC** fits into the world of libraries and their patrons.

> *People have needs.* We are going to concentrate on their *educational, informational, and recreational needs.*
>
> *Libraries collect materials.* These materials can satisfy the educational, informational, and recreational needs of some people.
>
> *People and library materials need to get together.* People who go to the library to satisfy their educational, informational, and recreational needs are called *library patrons.*

Somehow, we have to get our library materials organized so that patrons can find what they need. We have to get our materials under **bibliographic control.**

To find our materials, patrons must have the ability to search our library collections. In the distant past, the only way that patrons could search our collections was to physically scan our shelves of books and other **items.** People still use this approach to find materials in bookstores, and occasionally patrons will browse through the shelves of our libraries hoping that serendipity will provide them with the item that they need.

Eventually, however, we began to realize that shelf browsing was becoming too inefficient, as many library collections grew to be too large to be physically searched by a patron. We began to create lists or catalogs instead, with descriptions of the items in our collections.

The idea was that these **library catalogs** would provide specific information (called **bibliographic information**) about the materials in our library collections,

Fig. 1-1 ▪ A MARC Record

```
000     00876cam 2200277 a 4500
001        00123456
003     DLC
008     001023t20001999jm a    db   001 0 eng
Entrd: 001023       DtSt: t  Dates: 2000, 1999   Ctry: jm  Ills: a
Audn:      Form: d  Cont: b  GPub:      Conf: 0    Fest: 0
Indx: 1  M/E:      LitF: 0  Biog:       Lang: eng  MRec:    Srce:
010     ‡a   00123456
020     ‡a0805205569
040     ‡aDLC‡cDLC‡dDLC
050     ‡aF1872‡b.F8
100 1   ‡aFoster, Deb.
245 10  ‡aJamaica mine‡h[text (large print)] :‡bcataloging on an
          island /‡cby Deb and Rick Foster.
246 30  ‡aCataloging on an island
250     ‡a1st ed.
260     ‡aKingston, Jamaica :‡bCHOC,‡c2000, c1999.
300     ‡a93 p. :‡bill. ;‡c24 cm. +‡e1 videocassette (60 min. :
          sd., col. ; 1/2 in.)
440  0  ‡aCaribbean culture series
490 1   ‡aIslands in the sun
504     ‡aIncludes bibliographical references and index.
651  0  ‡aJamaica‡xDescription and travel.
651  0  ‡aJamaica‡xSocial conditions.
650  0  ‡aCataloging‡zJamaica.
700 1   ‡aFoster, Rick.
710 2   ‡aCatalogers Helping Other Catalogers, Inc.
800 1   ‡aFoster, Deb.‡tIslands in the sun.
```

and patrons could then decide from this information whether the physical items might meet their educational, informational, and recreational needs. This meant that instead of having to physically hunt through our shelves for materials, patrons could explore our collections by searching our catalogs to see the descriptions of our materials.

Not long ago we put these descriptions on three-by-five-inch catalog cards, filed in alphabetical order in long, wooden drawers; patrons searched our collections by flipping through the cards. When a patron found a card that seemed to describe an item that met his needs, he would jot down the **call number** from the card in the **card catalog** and go to look for the item in the stacks.

Now, many libraries have switched to using **computer catalogs** to provide the bibliographic information. Whether it is on a catalog card or in a **computer record,** however, it is the same information that we provide. And the purpose of that information is the same—to fulfill the objectives outlined by Charles Ammi Cutter back in 1876 (Cutter 1904):

> To enable a person to find a book [or video, electronic resource, etc.] of which the author, the title, or the subject is known.
>
> To show what the library has by a given author, on a given subject, or in a given kind of literature.
>
> To assist in the choice of a book [or sound recording, map, etc.] by its edition (bibliographically) or by its character (literary or topical).

Looking at the big picture, inside the library, where does the catalog—which makes library material accessible to patrons—fit in?

Here is an overview (albeit a cataloger's overview) of what we do in a library:

1. We choose materials.
2. We order materials.
3. We process materials.
4. We pay for materials.
5. We catalog materials.
6. We label materials.
7. We shelve materials.
8. We circulate materials.
9. We provide reference, **interlibrary loan,** and other services.

In other words, someone in the library:

1. chooses what the library will add to its collection (collection development);
2. orders the materials identified in step 1 (acquisitions);
3. unpacks and processes the ordered materials when they arrive and adds **barcode labels,** dust jackets, sturdy videocassette cases, etc. (processing);
4. keeps track of receipts and pays for these materials (accounting);
5. provides bibliographic information about these materials for the library's catalog (cataloging);
6. prints the call number created in step 5 on a label and affixes it to the new material (processing);
7. puts the new materials on the shelves in call number order (circulation);
8. checks materials out and (it is hoped) back in (circulation); and
9. provides access services: offers support services to help patrons find materials (reference), arranges for materials to be borrowed from and loaned to other libraries (ILL), and so on.

In step 5, cataloging, we create the bibliographic information that

describes the material;

provides terms by which a patron might search for the material (e.g., names, titles, subjects);

provides a call number so the material can be shelved with other materials on similar subjects (e.g., horses) or of the same physical medium (e.g., videos); and

links the barcode number from the new material to the **catalog record.**

Finally, to support all the preceding functions, most libraries now maintain **library automation systems** that include some or all of the following modules:

An acquisitions module for ordering and paying for materials (tasks 1, 2, 4)

A serials module for tracking receipt of periodicals (tasks 2, 4)

A cataloging module for entering bibliographic information (task 5)

An **online catalog** module for patrons and staff (task 9)

A circulation module for checking materials out and in (task 8)

At the core of the automated system is the bibliographic information that describes the materials in the library's collection and provides search terms so that these descriptions can be found. This bibliographic information is used not only by patrons searching for materials, but also by library staff when performing tasks 1–9.

In most automated systems in libraries today, this all-important bibliographic information is coded into a computer record using something called the **MARC format.**

There you have it: a very brief outline of the various library functions for which MARC is necessary. You will find these functions and their associated tasks being performed in every library in the land.

Some of you might work in large libraries and be familiar with only one of these functions. Some of you may be solo librarians and well acquainted with all these functions. Regardless, all these tasks are aimed at two very specific goals, the same goals we have had for many years:

To organize the library's materials

To provide the library's patrons with sufficient information so that they can find, identify, select, and obtain access to those materials (IFLA 2000)

QUIZ 1

Note: All quizzes are intended to be open-book. You are meant to find the appropriate answers in the preceding pages.

1. Which particular needs of people are we addressing in this book?

_____

2. How did people search our collections in the "very distant past" to find out whether we had materials that could meet those needs?

_____

3. How do patrons explore our collections now?

_____

4. What do we call the information that patrons are supposed to use to decide whether our materials will meet their needs?

_____

5. What format do we use to code this information in computer records for our automated systems?

_____

2

The Rules for Bibliographic Information and the Standards for MARC

Over the years, experts in the field of cataloging have come to the conclusion that it would be a good thing if all libraries everywhere would provide the same bibliographic information about the same materials. These experts have, with much squabbling, developed some comprehensive rules about precisely what elements this bibliographic information should contain, and how we can achieve consistency in providing that information.

These rules have changed (and continue to change) over time, and not every library follows the same rules worldwide. The current, nationally accepted **cataloging rules** for the United States, Great Britain, Canada, Australia, and most other English-speaking countries are called the *Anglo-American Cataloguing Rules,* or **AACR2.** These cataloging rules tell the cataloger how to describe and provide consistent search terms for the materials in our library collections (AACR 1998, 1).

The cataloging rules are amazingly comprehensive and contain such minute details as

> where to look on an item for the data that we can use to describe that item (e.g., do we take the title from the **title page** or from the dust jacket?)

> how to be consistent in our search terms (e.g., do we use Muhammad Ali or Cassius Clay as a **heading** for the boxer?)

> the punctuation that we are to use between different elements in the description

Using the cataloging rules, we know how to describe library holdings, but AACR2 isn't enough to get these descriptions into the online catalogs of today—for that we need MARC.

The official documentation describes MARC as "a carrier for bibliographic information" (*MARC21 Concise* 1999, introd.). It further states that this "MARC format is a standard for the representation and exchange of bibliographic data in machine-readable form." You need to understand that MARC does *not* tell us *how* to describe library materials; AACR2 does that. MARC, on the other hand, is the standard that has been developed for coding our bibliographic information into a computer record. To put it another way, MARC provides a vehicle for us to communicate bibliographic data electronically between libraries, and AACR2 provides the universally agreed-upon rules for the content of the MARC records (Gorman 2001). In short, MARC is a standard for entering bibliographic information into a computer record.

We have established that there are two separate sets of rules, or standards, involved in bibliographic information: one for describing library materials (AACR2), and one for representing these descriptions in our online catalogs (MARC).

With this in mind we are going to take a quick look at some of the most basic rules for providing bibliographic information.

The cataloging rules (AACR2) say that first we are to describe the material. Think about these six **areas of information:**

1. Title and statement of responsibility
2. Edition
3. Publication details
4. Physical description of the material
5. Series
6. Notes

This is called **bibliographic description.**

Why do we need so much detail? Although it is true that at the most basic level, many of our patrons won't care about more than an author and a title, others just might need more details, such as:

> Large print? This is important in a place like Florida.
>
> Illustrations? Someone might need a picture of a lion, so we say whether a book is illustrated.
>
> Illustrated by whom? Maybe someone needs the Dickens with the illustrations by Boz, and we had better not present her with the edition without illustrations, or with different illustrations. She needs that particular edition, and we need to be sure that if we say we have it, we really do have it and not some other "close enough" edition.

The following questions illustrate other possibly useful information:

> I'm doing a book report—how many pages does this book have?
>
> Which edition is it? First? Second? Fifty-second?
>
> Are there any bibliographies to help me find other stuff on this subject?

So we describe the material, as accurately as possible and in detail, because these days many of our patrons will be looking at these descriptions via computers. Some of our patrons may be homebound while others might be just too busy to make it to the library. Some of our patrons are interlibrary loan (ILL) patrons, and they could be thousands of miles away for all we know. Although it is wonderful that we can now allow patrons to search our collections from their computers at their convenience, this definitely increases our responsibility to make sure that our electronic descriptions truly represent the items in our collections. We certainly do not want to send the patron who is thousands of miles away something other than what we say we have.

It is imperative, therefore, that wherever our patrons may be, they can tell from our descriptions whether we have exactly what they are looking for. That is why we make our descriptions detailed and accurate: *so that our patrons can tell from the computer screen whether we really have what they want.*

One more reason for us to provide accurate descriptions is so that other catalogers can tell from our records whether they have the same items that we do. We will say more about this when we get to the concept of **copy cataloging.**

The cataloging rules (AACR2) then say to provide searchable terms, such as:

1. Author
2. Title
3. **Series**
4. **Added entries,** such as editors, related authors, related titles, etc.

These are called headings or **access points.**

We turn to AACR2 for instructions on when to provide the preceding four types of headings and how to be consistent in what we use for those headings.

Sometimes it is difficult to know what to call someone or something. Is he "John J. Smith" or "John James Smith"? Is it the "14th International Conference on AIDS" or the "14th International AIDS Conference"? It makes a difference. Do I call this thing a "bomb" or an "incendiary device"? Once we decide on a name for a heading, it's best to stick to that name. This is called making an **established heading,** and it is a key ingredient in our effort toward achieving bibliographic control.[1]

Try to imagine searching a multiplicity of library **databases** without this consistency, this control. It would be just like the Web, with everybody calling the same things by different names! But in libraries, we have always felt the need to organize information. Established headings are one way in which we provide this organization. It takes work, of course, but by being consistent in what we use for headings across all our library catalogs, we are able to ensure that a patron can find everything we have by a particular author or with a specific title and so on, no matter which library catalog the patron might be searching.

Subject headings are a special type of heading, and AACR2 does not cover them. To make consistent terminology possible for subject headings we use standardized lists of valid headings, referred to as **controlled vocabularies** and **thesauri.**

Most libraries now use LCSH **(Library of Congress Subject Headings)** as their source of subject headings. The following are some examples of LC subject headings (*Library of Congress Subject Headings* 2001).

Airplanes

Education—Great Britain—Colonies

Birthday cakes

Labor laws and legislation

World War, 1939–1945

Some smaller public and school libraries use the **Sears List of Subject Headings** instead of LCSH, but as we continue to strive for consistency across library catalogs, even small libraries are switching to LCSH. Some libraries supplement LCSH with other subject schemes, such as MeSH (**Medical Subject Headings** from the National Library of Medicine), LC's **Annotated Card Program Subject Headings, Canadian Subject Headings,** or the **Guidelines on Subject Access to Individual Works of Fiction, Drama, Etc.** (gsafd). Libraries with special collections often rely on a specialized thesaurus to give more detailed subject access to their materials.

Some catalogers create their own local subject headings when no existing scheme gives them the terms they need. This is perfectly permissible, as long as the catalogers indicate that those headings are local, and follow the general rules in the **Subject Cataloging Manual** for creating those headings (*Subject Cataloging Manual* 2000). We will learn how to indicate the sources used for subject headings in chapter 9.

After assigning subject headings, we then have to *classify* the material. We use **classification systems,** such as **Dewey Decimal Classification**—DDC (Dewey 1996) or **Library of Congress Classification**—LCC (*LC Classification Schedules*) to create the call numbers that we put on library materials. The purpose of this classification process is to group similar materials together on the shelves. Most academic libraries tend to use LCC, most public and school libraries tend to use DDC, and there are libraries, especially outside North America, that use other schemes, such as the **Universal Decimal Classification** (UDC).

Why do we have to follow so many complicated rules and schemes? Not everyone likes these rules, and they are admittedly rather complex and take some practice to learn. In fact, in the old days, some catalogers simply made up their own rules, since no one outside their own libraries would ever know or care. But that was in the old days.

The fact is that libraries are no longer islands unto themselves, and now that we have opened our collections to the outside world via the Internet, it is even more important than ever that we follow the rules. *It is especially imperative that we be consistent in our MARC records—the "carriers" of our bibliographic information.*

Why do we need to be so consistent? Here are two good reasons:

1. *MARC allows us to share records.* Before we had MARC records, it was difficult and time-consuming to use copy cataloging from other sources. Now that we have MARC records we no longer have to create all our records from scratch. If catalogers all follow the same rules and standards when they make records, then they can use each other's records. This is important because creating and maintaining the library database are the largest library expense after the collection itself.

2. *MARC allows us to share resources.* Before we had MARC records it was difficult and time-consuming to borrow materials from other libraries. Now that we have MARC records, we can easily find out what materials other libraries own and request that those materials be sent to us for the use of our patrons. **Union catalogs** (like OCLC) represent the collections of thousands of different libraries in one huge database; patrons can search OCLC and then request materials from any of the libraries represented in the database. **Virtual union catalogs** perform the same function by linking the databases of different libraries online, and patrons can request mate-

rials from any of the libraries represented in the linked databases. If we do not use the MARC format for our computer records, we will not be able to add them to a union database, virtual or otherwise. However, if we make our records MARC and follow the same cataloging rules for the data in the records, then our records can be combined with other MARC records in other databases.

The bottom line is that we follow rules because they help our patrons. So we use AACR2 (and the other rules that we mentioned earlier) to tell us what bibliographic information to provide. Then we turn to the MARC standards to tell us how to code this bibliographic information into the computer. For example, as illustrated in figure 2-1, chapter 2 of AACR2 tells us what information we need to provide to describe a book, then MARC tells us how to code that information:

Fig. 2-1 ■ From Rules to MARC

Cataloging Rules		MARC
2.1	Title and statement of responsibility area	245
2.2	Edition area	250
2.2	Material specific designation area (N/A)	
2.4	Imprint area	260
2.5	Physical description area	300
2.6	Series area	4XX
2.7	Notes area	5XX

It is, of course, possible to make MARC records without knowing AACR2 or any of the other cataloging rules, but whether these records will be of use to anyone beyond the confines of one's own library is another matter. Such records will not mesh seamlessly with the records from other libraries. This will make it difficult for patrons to determine if the materials represented by different records are the same or truly different, which will make it that much more difficult for patrons to find what they need.

It is also possible to follow the cataloging rules and provide bibliographic information in a machine-readable **format** other than MARC. But then we would be unable to share these records with other libraries, and, thus, we would be unable to share our resources. And if a new machine-readable format is ever selected to take the place of MARC, the same general principles will still apply—the new format will need to become a standard that all libraries can follow, so that we can continue to share our data and our resources. There's just no getting away from rules and standards in this line of work.

QUIZ 2

1. What are the six main "areas of information" that we provide for patrons when we describe material?

    _____

    _____

    _____

2. What are these "areas of information" called?

    _____

3. Why do we need to make our descriptions so detailed and accurate?

    _____

4. What four types of information do we provide so that patrons can search by them?

    _____

    _____

    _____

5. What is this searchable information called?

    _____

6. What do we call the process of "establishing" headings and providing "cross-references"?

    _____

7. AACR2 tells us what _____ to provide, then

    MARC tells us how to _____ that information for a

    _____.

8. Why do we need all these rules and standards?

    _____

Note

   1. So you say to yourself, "I think I'll establish this thing's name as a 'bomb.' But just in case someone is thinking of it as an 'incendiary device,' I'll create a **cross-reference** that leads from the heading that I didn't use to the one that I did use." This concept of establishing headings (always using the same name or term to refer to the same person or thing) and providing cross-references from variant forms is, in a nut-shell, called **authority work.**

3

MARC21 Records:
What Are They,
Why Do We Need Them, and
How Do We Get Them?

We have established that:

> patrons have educational, informational, and recreational needs;
>
> libraries provide patrons with bibliographic information about our materials—in the form of a catalog—so that they (the patrons) can determine whether or not our materials meet their needs;
>
> we must follow certain rules and standards when we provide this bibliographic information so that there will be consistency in the information provided in all library catalogs.

Now it is time to learn a bit more about how we came to put the bibliographic information into MARC records.

Background

The **Library of Congress** (LC) developed the MARC format. Very early on, in the beginning days of computers (the late 1960s), certain people at LC recognized the benefits that computerization could offer to the library catalog. LC brought together a broad segment of the library community under the leadership of Henriette Avram (the mother of MARC) to design the elements that should be present in a machine-readable catalog record.

LC and the National Library of Canada (NLC) keep MARC going. Currently, the Network Development and MARC Standards Office at LC and the Standards and Support Office at NLC maintain the MARC21 standards—the specific standards used by the United States, Canada, and other countries (*MARC Development* 2001). All MARC21 users, including **bibliographic utilities, library networks,** library automation system vendors, and libraries from around the world, provide input about these standards. LC maintains the MARC Forum, an electronic discussion list to facilitate discussion among all interested parties (MARC Forum 2001). The archives of this list can be found at the MARC website maintained by the Library of Congress (*MARC Standards* 2001).

Open sessions are held at the semiannual meetings of two special MARC committees, called "MARBI" **(Machine-Readable Bibliographic Information Committee)** in the United States and "CCM" **(Canadian Committee on MARC)** in Canada. These meetings are very well attended by many interested parties, and the views expressed at these meetings, along with others contributed via e-mail and the MARC Forum list, are used by LC and NLC to make final decisions about any needed changes to MARC.

That is another important thing about MARC: it constantly changes! In fact, it is quite possible that by the time you read this book, some element of MARC that we mention may have been changed and may now be **obsolete coding. Catalogers** and systems staff, therefore, need a way to keep up with those changes. The MARC Forum is a good way to do this, and it is particularly useful for informing us about upcoming proposed changes and for giving us access to the experts to ask for clarification about tricky coding.

Now let's get down to the nitty-gritty of MARC.

What Are MARC Records?

The term *MARC* stands for: *MA*chine *R*eadable *C*ataloging, but you should be aware that not all machine-readable cataloging records are MARC records.

Many records are still out there in library catalogs that are not in the MARC format. If the data has not been entered using the MARC coding standards that we will be looking at soon, then the records are not MARC records.

So, what are MARC records? The most important thing to remember about them is that they are computer records, created according to a very specific set of standards, designed for "identifying, storing, and communicating cataloging information" (Crawford 1989).

Because the concept of "communicating" cataloging records was central to the design of the MARC format, it is sometimes called the **MARC communications format.**

Also bear in mind that not all MARC formats are the same, and the names used to designate particular MARC formats change with time:

- LCMARC (1960s) = USMARC (1980s) = MARC21 (2000)
- CANMARC (1970s) = MARC21 (2000)

CANMARC (the Canadian version of MARC) started out as different from **LCMARC** (the American version of MARC), but after years of having to translate between records created using the slightly different standards, the two groups in charge of setting those standards finally decided to harmonize their MARCs, creating MARC21. A similar decision has been made regarding **UKMARC** (the British version of MARC) to make it, too, the same as MARC21. Before too much longer, therefore, UKMARC will also equal MARC21.

On the other hand, UNIMARC, IberMARC, NORMARC, and many other national MARCs are still not quite the same as MARC21. Records created using these formats still have to be translated into MARC21 in order for them to be used by software that is expecting to see MARC21 codes. Unless you live in a country that uses one of those other MARCs, however, you will probably never see a record in one of those other formats unless you specifically go looking for them, so concentrate on MARC21.

However, there is another format about which you should be aware, called **MicroLIF.** The designers of the PC-based library automation systems, such as Follett and Winnebago, decided that the complicated underlying structure of MARC was inappropriate for their platform. They came up with their own MARC-like standard that they called MicroLIF. The problem was that the records created using the MicroLIF standard were just different enough that systems built on LCMARC choked on the MicroLIF records. Eventually, the MicroLIF people gave up *saying* MicroLIF was just like MARC and joined the MARC community. The resulting version of MicroLIF is called **MicroLIF91.** If you are ever asked in which flavor you would prefer your records to be provided to you, MicroLIF or MicroLIF91, make sure you say MicroLIF91. All you need to remember is that Old MicroLIF is not MARC, but MicroLIF91 = MARC21.

Why Do We Need MARC Records?

Now that you know that not all MARCs are the same, you also need to know that not all MARC21 records are the same. We currently have five different types of MARC21 records. We will begin with the three most commonly used.

1. **MARC21 bibliographic records** provide descriptions of the materials that we collect and give access to those descriptions; that is, they contain bibliographic information.

2. **MARC21 authority records** provide established headings and cross references; that is, they are used for **authority control.**

3. **MARC21 holdings records** provide **holdings information** about individual items; that is, they contain barcode numbers, call numbers, volume/part/ year information, notes, etc.

We need these three different MARC21 records to keep track of each book, video, etc. that we collect in our libraries. For each item that we have, we need:

> One **bibliographic record** to *describe* the item and give headings for *access.*
>
> One **authority record** *for each heading* in the bibliographic record.
>
> One **holdings record** *for each copy or volume* of the item that we have.[1]

Not every library provides authority records at this time, so you may not have encountered them yet. Authority records register our decision when we establish a heading. In an authority record for a personal name, for example, we enter the name that we have established as the heading for the person; we also enter (as cross-references) any other names that have been used (or may be likely to be used) for that person, along with notes about our decisions that we think may be important.

Establishing headings and providing cross-references (*see* **references** and *see also* **references**) make it easier for patrons to find our materials, so we hope that more libraries will venture into this new realm of service as time goes on.

You may also never have seen a holdings record, because most library automation systems currently import and export holdings information using special fields in the bibliographic records, rather than using MARC holdings records. This lack of standards in holdings records is a problem when libraries switch systems, as anyone involved in a system migration can tell you. For this reason, libraries are beginning to require that their automation systems be able to create holdings records in the MARC21 holdings format.

Two other **MARC21 formats** are also available, although they are not as common as the previous three:

1. *MARC21 community information records* contain information about community events and organizations. You would use this format if you wanted to put local community information into your catalog along with the books, videos, sound recordings, etc.

2. *MARC21 classification records* contain information about classification numbers, so that classification schemes like LCC and DDC can be made available online as well as in print. This is not where you put call numbers; call numbers go in special fields in bibliographic records or holdings records. It is possible that these records may be used to check the validity of call numbers in a type of authority control. You may never have to deal directly with this format.

The coding in these different types of MARC21 records is similar in many ways, but there are sufficient differences to make the records very distinct. This means that you can never assume that a code in a MARC21 bibliographic record will have the same meaning in a MARC21 authority record. Unfortunately, we are not going to be able to get into coding for authority records at all in this book. We are going to have to concentrate on coding for bibliographic records because they are the ones that most people are concerned about.

We realize that this is starting to sound more and more complicated, so you may be asking once again why we need MARC records. Here are the two reasons we mentioned earlier:

1. *MARC allows sharing of records.* There are tens of millions of MARC records available for copying, so if you use MARC, you won't have to make your own original records for every item in your collection.

2. *MARC allows sharing of resources.* Because MARC records from all sorts of libraries can be put into the same union catalog (e.g., OCLC) or linked in a virtual catalog, it has become relatively easy to do ILL (interlibrary loaning). If you use MARC, you can participate in this **resource sharing** bonanza.

And now we add two new reasons for pursuing MARC records:

3. *MARC is a standard.* Most library automation systems are designed around the MARC standards. If you use MARC, you will be able to move your database—your most important investment after your collection—from one library system to another without having to convert every record into a new format every time you change systems. This is very important, given that most libraries will switch library systems every five or so years.

4. *MARC is easy to learn,* if you are taught it and not left to learn it on your own. (We admit that this is hard for some people to believe.)

How Do We Get MARC Records?

So how do we get MARC bibliographic records? We can get them either by making them from scratch ourselves (using the cataloging software in our library system) or by copy cataloging—and in the cataloging world, copying is perfectly acceptable and no one will accuse you of cheating!

In the "old days," copy cataloging was by no means a simple process. The primary union catalog available was something called the NUC **(National Union Catalog),** which was a catalog of the combined collections of the major research libraries in the United States and Canada. The NUC was composed of hundreds of huge green volumes that contained tiny copies of the shelflist cards of the major libraries. This meant that if your library was so lucky as to have the space to shelve the NUC, your catalogers could use it to find records that they could copy, and your ILL people could use it to find materials that they could borrow. This saved considerable intellectual effort, but the information on the tiny card facsimiles still had to be retyped at each library.

Then LC discovered computers and developed MARC and the next thing they knew, they could run off multiple sets of cards from the same computer record, instead of having to typeset those cards. Before we all got on the MARC bandwagon, therefore, libraries were already benefiting from MARC because they could do copy cataloging by ordering card sets from LC, saving not only intellectual labor, but also typing.

It wasn't long before the big libraries, which have always sought ways of making the cataloging process faster, cheaper, and better, decided that they needed to replace the National Union Catalog (paper or microfiche) with a MARC-based, computerized union catalog. From this initiative, **OCLC** and **RLG** (in the United States), and the now defunct WLN (in the United States), and **Utlas** (in Canada) were born. The intent behind these bibliographic utilities was to coordinate **cooperative cataloging.** The first cataloger to make a MARC record for an item would follow standard cataloging rules and coding in an effort to make the best record possible. Then that record would be added to the union catalog so that other catalogers could download a copy of that record and import it into their own library automation system.

Copy cataloging, therefore, is now considered to be the process of searching an outside source of MARC records; finding records that exactly match items in hand; possibly doing some editing to improve records; adding holdings information to records; **downloading records** from the source system; and **importing records** to one's library automation system. This may sound complicated, but it is a great deal easier than doing **original cataloging.**

For awhile, only large libraries that could afford to join the utilities could get access to MARC records from LC or other libraries for copy cataloging. Then a company called The Library Corporation got into the business of supplying MARC records from LC to everyone at a low cost, first on microfiche and then on CD-ROM. Now MARC records from LC and other libraries are available from a wide variety of sources.

Certainly you may still have to do original cataloging for some items, especially if you have local materials that no one else has. But always keep in mind that the only really cost-effective way to catalog nowadays is to first try to find records that you can copy.

Sources for Copying MARC Records: Free

Shared Systems

Sometimes a group of libraries will band together to share a library automation system. For example, ten separate public libraries might form a **library consortium** to purchase and maintain a library automation system, with a single **shared database** of MARC records. If you are part of a **shared system,** and another library in that system has already imported or created a MARC record that matches your item in hand, then you can simply attach the holdings information (barcode, call number, item cost, etc.) for your item to that MARC record, without having to copy or create a new record yourself. This is sometimes called **add item** or linking, but it is, in effect, copy cataloging just the same.

The Library of Congress

The reluctant de facto national library of the United States, the Library of Congress is still our largest single producer of MARC records. We can now go directly to the LC online catalog (http://catalog.loc.gov), search for records that match our titles, and copy (or "import") the records that we find there into the cataloging module of our own library automation system, free, gratis, at no charge.

What's the drawback, you ask? The online connection to LC is often overwhelmed by the number of libraries taking advantage of this boon. To cope with this, LC has a cap on the number of connections available at any given time. This means that you often may not be able to get through during U.S. business hours, and even when you do get through, you may find the connection is somewhat slow.

Direct access to the LC database of MARC records, therefore, may not be the most efficient way to get MARC records. It is, however, sometimes the *only* way a small library can afford to do copy cataloging.

Sources for Copying MARC Records: Not Free

Bibliographic Utilities

You must be a member of a bibliographic utility (for example, RLIN at http://www.rlg.org or OCLC at http://www.oclc.org) in order to get full access to all the cataloging functions of that utility. These utilities are, however, beginning to provide restricted copy cataloging access to their records for nonmembers, and this avenue may be worth investigating for smaller libraries.

Membership in a bibliographic utility is by no means inexpensive, but the utilities have gathered some impressive collections of records. For example, OCLC currently has over 50 million unique MARC records, compared to LC's 12 million. For many libraries, it is more cost-effective to pay a utility's fees in order to get prompt access to a large number of records and thus speed up the cataloging process.

In addition, the bibliographic utilities do more than just provide MARC records. Because so many libraries use them for copy cataloging, the utilities have found that if their member libraries add their library codes to each record that they copy, the resulting databases of shared records can also act as a union catalog for interlibrary loan. This means that your patrons can find and borrow not only the materials that you have in your own library collection, but also materials from the collections of other libraries participating in the union catalog.

MARC Record Vendors

As mentioned earlier, The Library Corporation was one of the first companies to make Library of Congress MARC records available to libraries for copying. The company began doing so using microfiche (just think of the eyestrain!) and then moved on to providing the actual MARC records from LC on CD-ROM. Their DOS-based cataloging software, Bibliofile, made it easy and efficient to search the entire LC database. Long before there was direct access to the LC database via the Internet, many smaller libraries were using Bibliofile to copy and edit matching LC records and download them into their automated systems. Many other vendors now also offer CD-ROM and/or Internet access to their copies of the LC database, sometimes along with MARC records that they have collected from various other sources.

Why do these vendors continue to do good business if we can get MARC records free from the same source that they do (LC)? Remember the limitations of going directly to LC that we mentioned earlier. Using a vendor's copy of the LC database online or on a CD-ROM guarantees a consistent response time, plus the vendor's software adds the ability to edit the records before they are imported to your system, something you cannot do if you go directly to LC.

Z39.50 Software

Z39.50 is another important standard for libraries. The **Z39.50 protocol** makes it possible for a library system that is designed by one vendor to execute a search on a completely different library system and retrieve MARC records for the search results. Don't worry, you don't have to learn Z39.50. You just need to know that if the cataloging module of your automation system implements the Z39.50 standard—and many do these days—then you can probably use that interface to search the databases of hundreds of library systems that also have Z39.50 interfaces and download MARC records from those databases. And if your library system does not have this Z39.50 capability (or if you do not have a library system), then you can buy stand-alone software that will run on your PC and perform the same search and retrieval functions.

Outsourcing

Finally, if your organization does not have the resources to do any cataloging at all, even copy cataloging, or if you cannot find MARC records to copy for some of the materials that you collect, then you might turn to **outsourcing** some or all of your cataloging. In this context, *outsourcing* simply means that you pay someone else to create your MARC records for you.

One type of outsourcing is to get your MARC records from your materials supplier. Many smaller libraries receive a MARC record for every item that they purchase; this service was provided initially by book jobbers, such as Baker & Taylor, Follett, and Brodart, but now even some publishers provide it. This situation is very similar to that in the "old days," when libraries would get card sets with the materials they purchased. And, as in the old days, the same issues of quality and accuracy must be faced. This means that someone in the library must still know enough about cataloging and MARC to know when the records being supplied are correct and when they are most decidedly not.

Another type of outsourcing is to send your library materials to a special cataloging vendor to have MARC records created for them. Some libraries simply do not have the staff to handle any cataloging at all; others do not have the resources to cope with the cataloging of a certain type of material, or of materials in a certain language, and so on. Even when you opt for this not inexpensive option, however, someone in the library must still know enough about cataloging and MARC to monitor the work done by the outsourcing vendor.

Quality Control

Wherever your MARC records come from, we cannot emphasize too much the need for quality control of those records. No matter from whence they originate (even from LC), you must ensure that your records are as complete and as accurate as possible, and that they are coded correctly. If your records aren't in very good shape (e.g., if they are riddled with **invalid coding**), then your system will not work very well. It's that simple.

We have heard it said over and over again by staff from many different libraries that they have neither the time nor, often, the inclination to learn MARC— much less the cataloging rules. This is unfortunate, because although they may be doing "the best they can," they probably are making catalog records that will not properly fulfill the functions of a catalog (which we are going to cover in more detail in the next chapter).

If you don't have time to do it right the first time, you must have time to do it over again.

—ANONYMOUS

In order to be useful, catalog records must provide "the library patrons with sufficient information so that they can find, identify, select, and obtain access" to a library's materials (IFLA 2000). Records with inadequate or inaccurate bibliographic information and improper MARC coding will limit the ability of patrons, whether local or via ILL, to "find, identify, select, and obtain access" to materials.

When libraries come out of their isolation to join the resource-sharing community, they often find that their original records are unsuitable for sharing purposes. This means that they will only be able to share records that they have copied from other libraries, and their homemade records—for their most valuable materials, the unique items that only they hold—will not be suitable for union catalogs like OCLC, and also will not work well in a virtual union catalog. In today's record-sharing environment, therefore, it is becoming more obvious than ever that there is hardly any point in doing cataloging at all, unless it is done according to the rules and standards.

QUIZ 3

1. Where was MARC first developed?

_____

2. Are all machine-readable cataloging records MARC records?

    [ ] Yes   [ ] No

3. Is UNIMARC the same as MARC21?

   [   ] Yes   [   ] No

4. Has MARC21 changed since it was first set up in the 1960s?

   [   ] Yes   [   ] No

5. Do all the codes in a MARC21 bibliographic record have the same meaning in a MARC21 authority record?

   [   ] Yes   [   ] No

6. How do we get MARC21 bibliographic records?

   _____

Note

1. Library automation systems also need a way to store information about patrons (barcode ID number, name, items checked out, etc.). Currently, no MARC format exists for **patron records,** and they are not really standardized in any way, so the format of these records varies from system to system.

4

MARC21 and the
Computerized Catalogs of Today

Before we get too deep into actual MARC coding, we should provide a quick review of how a library catalog works and what you can expect to see there.

Remember that the library catalog is a compilation of descriptions of the materials that we have in our library collections. A library catalog is intended to allow a patron to:

> find information about materials that we have in our library collections (via searching);
>
> use that information to decide if he or she wants to see the physical material (via displays);
>
> use that information to confirm whether the material is currently available.

To find our descriptions, patrons used to come into our libraries and flip through our catalog cards, a process called "browsing the catalog."

These catalog cards were organized alphabetically by the different types of headings that we provided:

> names
>
> titles
>
> subjects

These groups of headings can also be referred to as **indexes** (simply another name for lists arranged in alphabetical order). In some libraries the cards for names, titles, and subjects were interfiled in one place **(dictionary catalogs)**; in other libraries the cards for names and titles were kept separate from the cards for subjects **(divided catalogs).** In a large university library, it would not be unusual to have to go to another room to search the subject catalog.

These days, patrons do not *have* to come to our physical locations to search our catalogs; instead, they can sit at computers either in the library or at home and search for computer records in our **OPACs.** *OPAC* means Online Public Access Catalog, which is just a fancy name for our computer catalog. Some people call them **WebPACs** if they are available via the Internet.

We are going to briefly outline some options for searching a typical OPAC, using the one at the Library of Congress (LC) as an example. Then we will take a quick look at some of the various ways that different OPACs display the bibliographic information in MARC records for patrons and staff.

Figure 4-1 shows the opening screen of the OPAC at the Library of Congress (http://catalog.loc.gov) (viewed Feb. 2002). There are typically two ways to search an OPAC—**browse searching** and **keyword searching.**

Fig. 4-1 ■ Opening Screen of the Library of Congress OPAC

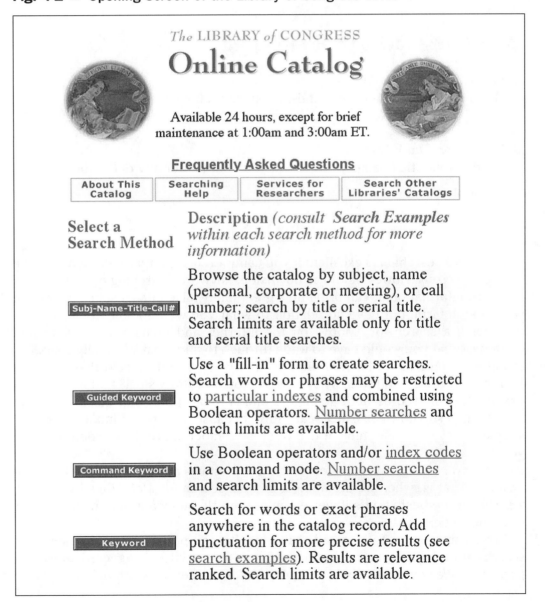

Browse searching is similar to searching catalog cards, because it relies on alphabetical lists of headings or indexes for:

names

titles

subjects

In browse searching, you first choose a specific type of index to search (usually either name, title, or subject). You then enter the *first word* or words of a heading, and the computer quickly scans ahead to that part of the index where the headings begin with the word entered.

When you are searching for a **keyword,** however, you can find any word anywhere in an **indexed field.** This is possible because the computer can index every word in every record in the catalog, if we set it up to do so. If a patron wants to search for a word that is not at the beginning of a heading, he or she can now perform a keyword search instead of a browse search.

Searching: Browse versus Keyword

Moby Dick, or, The Whale
To find this title in a browse index, you would have to enter:

Moby

Moby Dick, or, The Whale
To find this title in a keyword index, you could enter any of the following:

Moby

Dick

whale

Keyword searching is excellent if you cannot remember a title or a name or a subject precisely. However, on the downside, keyword searching often retrieves *too much* information. It can bring up a great many false hits (results that match your search term, but have no relation to what you were looking for). Just picture doing a search for "Moby" on the Internet and imagine how many hits (matches) that you would have to wade through to find what you really want. For example, Google found 534,000 hits on "Moby." (It could be said that keyword searches are always followed by a certain amount of "browsing," that is, repeated examination of records until a suitable one is found.) So don't discard browse searching (also known as **exact searching**) because it does not initially seem as simple as keyword searching. It can often be a much more direct route to what you seek.

Library catalogs also preserve the distinctions among different types of heading. That is, when we are doing a browse search for *Moby Dick* by its title, we will get the best results if we search in the title index and not in the subject or author index.

The same applies to keyword searching. We can perform a general keyword search, which looks for our search word in any indexed field in a record; or we can perform a *title* keyword search, which looks for our search word only in the title fields; a *name* keyword search, which looks for our search word only in the name fields; or a *subject* keyword search, which looks for our search word only in the subject fields.

For any of these kinds of searches to work, however, we must first have told our automated system to put specific data from our MARC records into the appropriate indexes. We will go into more detail about which data goes into which indexes in chapter 8. For now, just be aware that someone actually has to set up this indexing for the library's automated system—either the library automation system vendor or someone in the library.

Browse Searches at LC

Most, if not all, systems allow patrons to perform a browse search in a subject, name, or title index. As we can see from figure 4-2, at LC, patrons can also browse in separate indexes for serial titles and call numbers.

Fig. 4-2 ■ LC's Browse Menu

| Keyword | Subj-Name-Title-Call# | Guided Keyword | Command Keyword |

Database Name: Library of Congress Online Catalog
Note: Limits are only available for Title and Serial Title searches.

Search by:

○ Subject Browse ● Name Browse ○ Title ○ Serial Title ○ Call Number Browse

Enter search in box (see search examples):

    hoobler, dorothy

[Search] [Reset]

Keyword Searches at LC

Most, if not all, systems also allow patrons to perform keyword searches in a subject, name, or title index. LC provides these options in what is called *guided keyword* searching (see fig. 4-3). (Be aware that these **search screens** can and do change as libraries redesign their search options.)

Not all libraries offer as many separate keyword indexes as you will find at LC, but most give more than just a general keyword index (keyword anywhere) with everything dumped into one big pot. The capability of restricting a search to a specific index (or context) allows our patrons to do more precise searching than the search engines on the Internet provide.

Fig. 4-3 ▪ LC's Keyword Menu

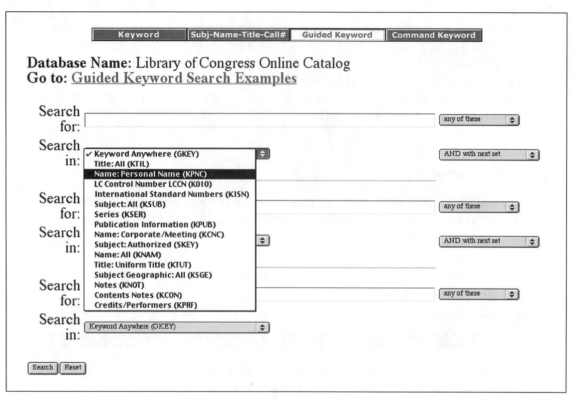

OPAC Displays

Once you have chosen your index and entered your search terms, the system scans through the chosen index and displays various levels of results. Let's look at some results for a browse search in the name index for "Hoobler, Dorothy."

LC's Name Browse List—First Level

Browse searching is not usually intended to retrieve a single item; rather, it is intended to place you at that point in the index where your search word(s) first occurs. Some OPACs, like LC's, position your search word at the top of the list. Figure 4-4 shows the results of a browse search for the name "Hoobler, Dorothy" at LC. This browse list shows us headings from the name index that begin with our search term; it indicates that this heading is a personal name, and tells us how many times each heading on the list occurs in our catalog. (Remember that a heading is something that we add to a description of an item because we believe that a patron is likely to search by it.)

Other OPACs position the heading that you searched in the middle of the screen, so that you can get an idea of the context—what comes just before and what comes just after the heading in the alphabetical listing.

Fig. 4-4 ■ A First-Level Browse List at LC

Database Name: Library of Congress Online Catalog
YOU SEARCHED: Name Browse = hoobler, dorothy
SEARCH RESULTS: Displaying 1 through 25 of 25.

◄ Previous   Next ►

#	Titles	Headings	Heading Type
1	72	Hoobler, Dorothy.	personal name
2	8	Hoobler, Icie Gertrude Macy, 1892-	personal name
3	1	Hoobler, James.	personal name
4	6	Hoobler, James A.	personal name
5	2	Hoobler, Sibley.	personal name
6	1	Hoobler, Sibley Worth, 1911-	personal name
7	74	Hoobler, Thomas.	personal name

LC's Name Browse Hitlist—Second Level

If we go back to the OPAC at LC and follow through with our search and choose "Hoobler, Dorothy" from the list, we are taken to a **hitlist** of titles by Dorothy, because "Hoobler, Dorothy" has more than one **work** in this database. These results (see fig. 4-5) list all the works by Dorothy in the LC catalog. (In library lingo,

Fig. 4-5 ■ A Second-Level Browse List at LC

YOU SEARCHED: Name Browse = hoobler, dorothy
SEARCH RESULTS: Displaying 1 through 25 of 72.

◄ Previous   Next ►

#	Name Heading	Name: Main Author, Creator, etc.	Full Title	Date
☐ 1	Hoobler, Dorothy.		Indoor gardening / by Dorothy and Thomas Hoobler ... [et al.].	1976
☐ 2	Hoobler, Dorothy.		Real American girls tell their own stories / [edited by] Dorothy and Thomas Hoobler.	1999
☐ 3	Hoobler, Dorothy.	Hoobler, Dorothy.	1920s : luck / by Dorothy and Tom Hoobler ; sketches by Alain Picard.	2000
☐ 4	Hoobler, Dorothy.	Hoobler, Dorothy.	1930s : directions / by Dorothy and Tom Hoobler.	2000

"hitlist" is not a Mafia term. A hitlist is an alphabetical list of "hits," or "matches," on a search.)

LC's Brief Record

Next, in the LC OPAC, if we choose the title *The 1930s: Directions* from the hitlist, we are then taken to a **brief record** (see fig. 4-6). Some patrons will need to look no farther than this brief record in order to tell whether this is the material they want. Others, however, may need more details.

Fig. 4-6 ■ A Brief Record at LC

Brief Record	Subjects/Content	Full Record	MARC Tags

The 1930s : directions / by Dorothy and Tom Hoobler.

LC Control Number: 00026513
 Type of Material: Book (Print, Microform, Electronic, etc.)
 Brief Description: Hoobler, Dorothy.
 The 1930s : directions / by Dorothy and Tom Hoobler.
 Brookfield, Conn. : Millbrook Press, c2000.
 159 p. : ill. ; 22 cm.

CALL NUMBER: PZ7.H76227 Aa 2000

LC's Full Record

When a patron needs more information, he or she can choose to display a more complete **full record** after seeing a brief record. Notice the OPAC labels down the left side of the screen in figure 4-7.

Displays in Different OPACs

Now you know how a hitlist, a brief record, and a full record display in the OPAC at LC. However, the very same hitlist, brief record, and full record will often look completely different in the OPAC of another library. That library might have a different library automation system, or it might have the same system as LC but decide to display the information in a different order and with different OPAC labels.

Also note that in order for any results to display, someone must have told the system what data from the MARC records to display in each type of the displays we have shown. This means that all displays can and do change as libraries experiment to find the best way to show information to their patrons.

A Full Record in The Mind

Figure 4-8 shows our very same record in the WebPAC catalog for the Pasco County (Florida) School System (viewed Feb. 2002). This display has different

Fig. 4-7 ■ A Full Record at LC

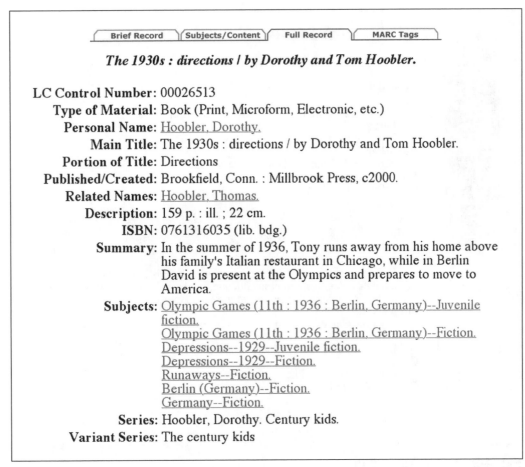

| Brief Record | Subjects/Content | Full Record | MARC Tags |

The 1930s : directions / by Dorothy and Tom Hoobler.

LC Control Number: 00026513

Type of Material: Book (Print, Microform, Electronic, etc.)

Personal Name: Hoobler, Dorothy.

Main Title: The 1930s : directions / by Dorothy and Tom Hoobler.

Portion of Title: Directions

Published/Created: Brookfield, Conn. : Millbrook Press, c2000.

Related Names: Hoobler, Thomas.

Description: 159 p. : ill. ; 22 cm.

ISBN: 0761316035 (lib. bdg.)

Summary: In the summer of 1936, Tony runs away from his home above his family's Italian restaurant in Chicago, while in Berlin David is present at the Olympics and prepares to move to America.

Subjects: Olympic Games (11th : 1936 : Berlin, Germany)--Juvenile fiction.
Olympic Games (11th : 1936 : Berlin, Germany)--Fiction.
Depressions--1929--Juvenile fiction.
Depressions--1929--Fiction.
Runaways--Fiction.
Berlin (Germany)--Fiction.
Germany--Fiction.

Series: Hoobler, Dorothy. Century kids.

Variant Series: The century kids

OPAC labels and a different order of data. For example, note that in the full record in The Mind, the title is listed before the author; whereas in the LC full record, the personal name is listed before the main title.

A Full Record in Alleycat

Figure 4-9 shows our record in the Alleycat catalog (viewed Feb. 2002), a virtual union catalog shared by a number of libraries in Florida. Again, notice the different OPAC labels and, in this case, that not all the same information is displayed.

Vendors

The list of vendors that provide library automation systems is a very long one, and it is beyond the scope of our book to go into them all. We just want to point out that each of these system vendors may have fundamentally different ideas about what patrons want to see. And again, not only will records on vendor A's system, for example, display quite differently in the OPAC than records on vendor B's system, but also records on two vendor A systems can display quite differently, depending on how the OPACs are set up by the library (because flexibility in the OPAC display is one of the features that the vendors use to sell their online catalogs to libraries).

Fig. 4-8 ■ A Full Record in The Mind

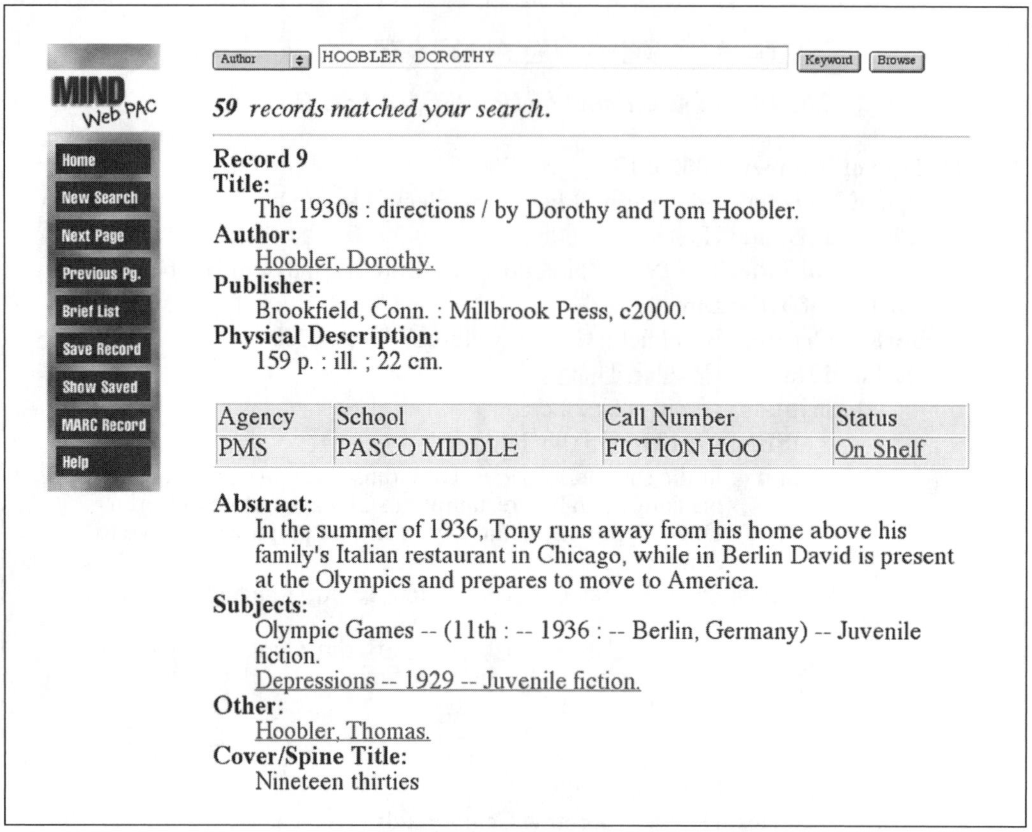

Author | HOOBLER DOROTHY | Keyword | Browse

59 records matched your search.

MIND Web PAC

Home
New Search
Next Page
Previous Pg.
Brief List
Save Record
Show Saved
MARC Record
Help

Record 9
Title:
The 1930s : directions / by Dorothy and Tom Hoobler.
Author:
Hoobler, Dorothy.
Publisher:
Brookfield, Conn. : Millbrook Press, c2000.
Physical Description:
159 p. : ill. ; 22 cm.

Agency	School	Call Number	Status
PMS	PASCO MIDDLE	FICTION HOO	On Shelf

Abstract:
In the summer of 1936, Tony runs away from his home above his family's Italian restaurant in Chicago, while in Berlin David is present at the Olympics and prepares to move to America.
Subjects:
Olympic Games -- (11th : -- 1936 : -- Berlin, Germany) -- Juvenile fiction.
Depressions -- 1929 -- Juvenile fiction.
Other:
Hoobler, Thomas.
Cover/Spine Title:
Nineteen thirties

Fig. 4-9 ■ A Full Record in Alleycat

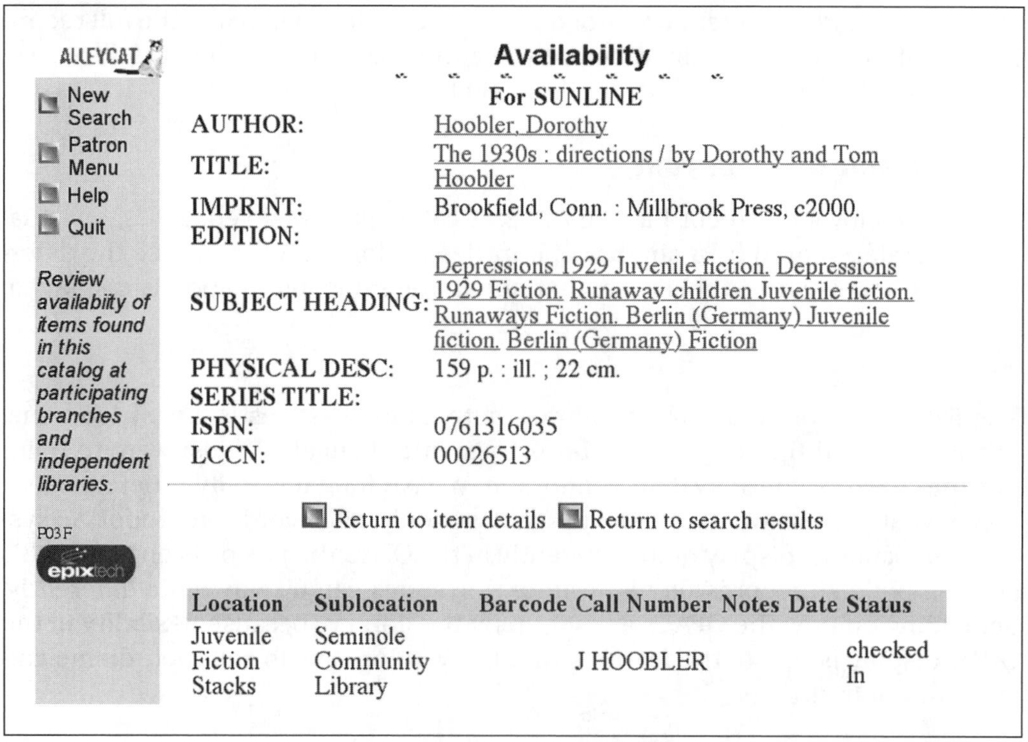

ALLEYCAT

New Search
Patron Menu
Help
Quit

Review availabity of items found in this catalog at participating branches and independent libraries.

P03F

epixtech

Availability

For SUNLINE

AUTHOR:	Hoobler, Dorothy
TITLE:	The 1930s : directions / by Dorothy and Tom Hoobler
IMPRINT:	Brookfield, Conn. : Millbrook Press, c2000.
EDITION:	
SUBJECT HEADING:	Depressions 1929 Juvenile fiction. Depressions 1929 Fiction. Runaway children Juvenile fiction. Runaways Fiction. Berlin (Germany) Juvenile fiction. Berlin (Germany) Fiction
PHYSICAL DESC:	159 p. : ill. ; 22 cm.
SERIES TITLE:	
ISBN:	0761316035
LCCN:	00026513

Return to item details Return to search results

Location	Sublocation	Barcode	Call Number	Notes	Date	Status
Juvenile Fiction Stacks	Seminole Community Library		J HOOBLER			checked In

Standardization

The flexibility in displays is fun for us, but is it good for our patrons? This is one of the blessings and curses of computer catalogs. When we had catalog cards, we tried very hard to ensure that every card in every library looked the same. Now we have computer catalogs, and none of our catalogs looks the same! What happened to standardization? This problem is partly a result of the novelty of computerized catalogs and partly a result of the medium itself. In the computer, unlike on the catalog card, the record display is not set in stone (or, rather, in print), and can easily be changed according to the fancy or judgment of the people responsible for each system.

Be that as it may, we still strive for consistency in the actual bibliographic information, which, as we have said before, is what the MARC record is all about. And even if the displays look different now, it is quite likely that as time goes on and the novelty wears off, we will devise a standardized display and return to the romantic ideal of allowing patrons to go from one library catalog to another and see displays that are comfortingly familiar.

The important thing to realize is that although these OPAC displays may look quite different, they are actually all based on the very same MARC record.

MARC Displays

Figure 4-10 is a MARC bibliographic record in its raw MARC communications format. The first twenty-four characters in bold (01518cam 2200373 a 4500) are called the **leader.** These characters tell the system important information about the record itself, not about what the record is describing.

The **directory** is the long set of numbers that follow the leader. These numbers tell the system which fields of data are present in a record, where each field

Fig. 4-10 ■ A Raw MARC Record

```
Technical Committee.п2 ‡aInstitute of Electrical and Electronics Engineers.
‡bPhiladelphia Section.п 01518cam  2200373 a
45000010009000000050017000090080041000260100017000670200002700084040000180011104200090
01290430012001380500002400150082001400174100002200188245005900210246001500269260000500
02843000029003344900021003635200188003846110072005726110063006446500041070765000320
07486500023007806510031008036510022008347000021008568000037008779060045009149250044∅
0959955014101003-11918876-20001107155416.0-000223s2000       ctua  c    000 1 eng -
‡a   00026513 -  ‡a0761316035 (lib. bdg.)-  ‡aDLC‡cDLC‡dDLC-  ‡alcac-  ‡ae-ge----00-
aPZ7.H76227‡bFo 2000-00‡a[Fic]‡221-1  ‡aHoobler, Dorothy.-14‡aThe 1930s :‡bdirections
/‡cby Dorothy and Tom Hoobler.-30‡aDirections-  ‡aBrookfield, Conn. :‡bMillbrook
Press,‡cc2000.-  ‡a159 p. :‡bill. ;‡c22 cm.-1 ‡aThe century kids-  ‡aIn the summer
of 1936, Tony runs away from his home above his family's Italian restaurant in
Chicago, while in Berlin David is present at the Olympics and prepares to move to
America.-20‡aOlympic Games‡n(11th :‡d1936 :‡cBerlin, Germany)‡vJuvenile fiction.-
21‡aOlympic Games‡n(11th :‡d1936 :‡cBerlin, Germany)‡vFiction.-
0‡aDepressions‡y1929‡vJuvenile fiction.- 1‡aDepressions‡y1929‡vFiction.-
1‡aRunaways‡vFiction.- 1‡aBerlin (Germany)‡vFiction.- 1‡aGermany‡vFiction.-1
‡aHoobler, Thomas.-1 ‡aHoobler, Dorothy.‡tCentury kidsп 01007cas  2200289 a
45000010013000000030004000130050017000170080041000340100017000750350020000920400000420
01120420008001540500002100162110002900183245005100212246003300262326000440029630000250
03403620019003655000032003846500051004166500037004676500047005046500057005517800091∅
0608850001800699пsn 92038078  пDLCп19930416121957.0п871125c19889999cauuu    c    0
0eng dп  ‡asn 92038078  п  ‡a(OCoLC)17064418п
‡aMWP‡cMWP‡dOCoLC‡dWaU‡dOCoLC‡dDLC‡dNSTп  ‡alcdп14‡aTK7870.3b.H485aп2 ‡aHewlett-
Packard Company.п10‡aTest &
```

begins, and how many characters each field contains. The remaining characters (in bold in fig. 4-10) contain the actual bibliographic information.

MARC records are designed to be wonderfully flexible. With MARC records, we can have:

> **variable-length fields,** which allow us to enter short titles like *Trees,* or longer titles like *The trees of North America and a guide to the major native and introduced species of Canada and Mexico;*

> **variable-length records,** which allow us to enter very short records (for example, for fiction books with few fields) or very long records (for example, for videos needing many notes fields).

No space is wasted and no field or record definitions need to be changed for longer or shorter records with this very efficient format. However, it cannot be denied that raw communications MARC records are confusing to look at, so systems convert this computer-friendly format into something more people-friendly, easier to read. Unfortunately, each system can, and usually does, display the MARC records differently. Let's take a look at some examples of different **MARC displays.**

LC can't seem to fit much on a screen in its online catalog. For some reason, LC's library automation system indents deeply and begins a new line for the subfields of each field (see fig. 4-11). MARC records are easier to read at LC when they are accessed via its Z39.50 interface. This display (see fig. 4-12) is much sim-

Fig. 4-11 ■ A MARC Display in the OPAC at LC

| Brief Record | Subjects/Content | Full Record | MARC Tags |

The 1930s : directions / by Dorothy and Tom Hoobler.

LC Control Number: 00026513

```
000 01518cam 2200373 a 4500
001 11918876
005 20011214144240.0
008 000223s2000 ctua c 000 1 eng
906 __
        |a 7 |b cbc |c orignew |d 1 |e ocip |f 20 |g y-gencatlg
925 0_
        |a acquire |b 2 shelf copies |x policy default
955 __
        |a to HLCD pc17 02-23-00; lb14 02-24-00; lb09
        04-25-00;lb05 04-26-00 to cip; CIP ver. pv08 to BCCD
        10-03-00; lc15 (copy 2) to BCCD 11-07-00
010 __
        |a 00026513
020 __
        |a 0761316035 (lib. bdg.)
040 __
        |a DLC |c DLC |d DLC
```

Fig. 4-12 ■ A Z39.50 MARC Display at LC

```
001 11918876
005 20011214144240.0
008 000223s2000    ctua    c       000 1 eng
906    $a7$bcbc$corignew$d1$eocip$f20$gy-gencatlg
925 0 $aacquire$b2 shelf copies$xpolicy default
955    $ato HLCD pc17 02-23-00; lb14 02-24-00; lb09 04-25-00;lb05 04-26-00 to
    cip; CIP ver. pv08 to BCCD 10-03-00; lc15 (copy 2) to BCCD 11-07-00
010    $a   00026513
020    $a0761316035 (lib. bdg.)
040    $aDLC$cDLC$dDLC
042    $alcac
043    $ae-ge---
050 00$aPZ7.H76227$bAa 2000
082 00$a[Fic]$221
100 1 $aHoobler, Dorothy.
245 14$aThe 1930s :$bdirections /$cby Dorothy and Tom Hoobler.
246 30$aDirections
260    $aBrookfield, Conn. :$bMillbrook Press,$cc2000.
300    $a159 p. :$bill. ;$c22 cm.
490 1 $aThe century kids
520    $aIn the summer of 1936, Tony runs away from his home above his family's
    Italian restaurant in Chicago, while in Berlin David is present at the
    Olympics and prepares to move to America.
650  0$aDepressions$y1929$vJuvenile fiction.
611 20$aOlympic Games$n(11th :$d1936 :$cBerlin, Germany)$vJuvenile fiction.
650  1$aDepressions$y1929$vFiction.
611 21$aOlympic Games$n(11th :$d1936 :$cBerlin, Germany)$vFiction.
651  1$aBerlin (Germany)$vFiction.
651  1$aGermany$vFiction.
650  1$aRunaways$vFiction.
700 1 $aHoobler, Thomas.
800 1 $aHoobler, Dorothy.$tCentury kids.
```

Labeled display | Brief Record Display | New Search

pler for a cataloger to use than the OPAC, both for searching and for the appearance of the MARC records.

Figure 4-13 shows the very same MARC record at OCLC, viewed using the Passport software. If you are a cataloging member of OCLC or use it for interlibrary loan, this display will be familiar to you.

We will say more about fields and subfields and fixed-length fields and indicators soon, but for now, just notice that the MARC display at OCLC looks different than the MARC display at LC. These are *not different records*, although they may each have some additional fields—they just *look* different.

Even though MARC records at OCLC look different when seen in the OCLC system, those records will look the same as records from any other source, once they are loaded to your own system.

Figure 4-14 shows the MARC display we are going to use throughout the rest of the book. Remember, MARC displays may look different, but the same MARC records have the same MARC data underneath, no matter how they look.

In the next chapter, we will cover the MARC terminology that you need in order to understand the following words. After you have read that chapter, come back to these examples of MARC records and notice the differences in:

the display of the *subfield delimiters;*

the spacing between *subfield codes* and punctuation, and between punctuation and data;

the line numbers that OCLC shows before the *tag* numbers.

Fig. 4-13 ■ A MARC Display at OCLC (viewed using Passport software)

```
OCLC: 43945178       Rec stat:  c
Entered:  20000223    Replaced:  20001109    Used:  20011015
Type: a   ELvl:     Srce:      Audn: c    Ctrl:     Lang: eng
BLvl: m   Form:     Conf: 0    Biog:      MRec:     Ctry: ctu
          Cont:     GPub:      LitF: 1    Indx: 0
Desc: a   Ills: a   Fest: 0    DtSt: s    Dates: 2000,    <
> 1 010     00-26513 <
         ...
>11 100 1  Hoobler, Dorothy. <
>12 245 14 The 1930s : ǂb directions / ǂc by Dorothy and Tom Hoobler. <
>13 246 30 Directions <
>14 260    Brookfield, Conn. : ǂb Millbrook Press, ǂc c2000. <
>15 300    159 p. : ǂb ill. ; ǂc 22 cm. <
>16 490 1  The century kids <
>17 520    In the summer of 1936, Tony runs away from his home above his
           family's Italian restaurant in Chicago, while in Berlin David is
           present at the Olympics and prepares to move to America. <
>18 650  0 Depressions ǂy 1929 ǂv Juvenile fiction. <
>19 611 20 Olympic Games ǂn (11th : ǂd 1936 : ǂc Berlin, Germany) ǂv
           Juvenile fiction. <
>20 650  1 Depressions ǂy 1929 ǂv Fiction. <
>21 611 21 Olympic Games ǂn (11th : ǂd 1936 : ǂc Berlin, Germany) ǂv
           Fiction. <
>22 651  1 Germany ǂv Fiction. <
>23 650  1 Runaways ǂv Fiction. <
>24 700 1  Hoobler, Thomas. <
>25 800 1  Hoobler, Dorothy. ǂt Century kids. <
```

Fig. 4-14 ■ A Generic MARC Record

```
000 01518cam 2200373 a 4500
001   00026513
003 DLC
008 000223s2000  ctua  c   000 1 eng
Entrd: 000223       DtSt: s   Dates: 2000,        Ctry: ctu  Ills: a
Audn: c   Form:     Cont:     GPub:     Conf: 0   Fest: 0
Indx: 0   M/E:      LFic: 1   Biog:     Lang: eng MRec:      Srce:
010     $a  00026513
020     $a0761316035 (lib. bdg.)
040     $aDLC$cDLC$dDLC
050 00  $aPZ7.H76227$bFo 2000
082 00  $a[Fic]$221
100 1   $aHoobler, Dorothy.
245 14  $aThe 1930s :$bdirections /$cby Dorothy and Tom Hoobler.
246 30  $aDirections
260     $aBrookfield, Conn. :$bMillbrook Press,$cc2000.
300     $a159 p. :$bill. ;$c22 cm.
490 1   $aThe century kids
520     $aIn the summer of 1936, Tony runs away from his home above his
        family's Italian restaurant in Chicago, while in Berlin David is
        present at the Olympics and prepares to move to America.
611 20  $aOlympic Games$n(11th :$d1936 :$cBerlin, Germany)$vJuvenile fiction.
611 21  $aOlympic Games$n(11th :$d1936 :$cBerlin, Germany)$vFiction.
650  0  $aDepressions$y1929$vJuvenile fiction.
650  1  $aDepressions$y1929$vFiction.
650  1  $aRunaways$vFiction.
651  1  $aGermany$vFiction.
700 1   $aHoobler, Thomas.
800 1   $aHoobler, Dorothy.$tCentury kids.
```

Notice also that OCLC does not show the delimiter and code for subfield $a. Finally, notice the different mnemonic labels that OCLC uses for the *fixed-field data* in its display compared to the mnemonic labels in the 008 in the generic display, and the lack of any mnemonic labels at all in the 008 of the LC display.

In the next chapter, we will also show you that the data that we put in these MARC records is very similar to the data that we used to put on library catalog cards.

Walt Crawford says that MARC is "a set of standards for identifying, storing, and communicating cataloging information" (Crawford 1989). That is just what catalog cards are also: a method of identifying, storing, and communicating cataloging (or bibliographic) information. And Michael Gorman says that MARC is "the electronic version of a catalogue card as a carrier of bibliographic data" (Gorman 2001). So, as you can see in figure 4-15, with MARC, we provide the same bibliographic information for our patrons that we did on cards, just in a somewhat different carrier!

Fig. 4-15 ■ From Catalog Cards to MARC

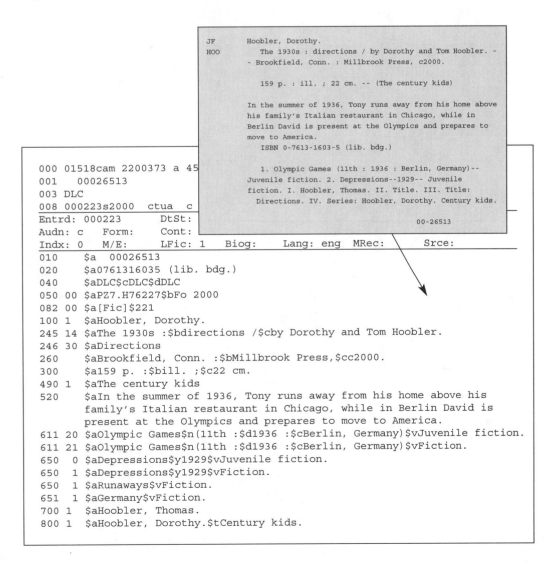

```
JF        Hoobler, Dorothy.
HOO          The 1930s : directions / by Dorothy and Tom Hoobler. -
          - Brookfield, Conn. : Millbrook Press, c2000.

             159 p. : ill. ; 22 cm. -- (The century kids)

          In the summer of 1936, Tony runs away from his home above
          his family's Italian restaurant in Chicago, while in
          Berlin David is present at the Olympics and prepares to
          move to America.
             ISBN 0-7613-1603-5 (lib. bdg.)

             1. Olympic Games (11th : 1936 : Berlin, Germany)--
          Juvenile fiction. 2. Depressions--1929-- Juvenile
          fiction. I. Hoobler, Thomas. II. Title. III. Title:
          Directions. IV. Series: Hoobler, Dorothy. Century kids.

                                              00-26513
```

```
000  01518cam 2200373 a 45
001    00026513
003 DLC
008 000223s2000   ctua  c
Entrd: 000223       DtSt:
Audn: c    Form:    Cont:
Indx: 0    M/E:     LFic: 1   Biog:    Lang: eng  MRec:      Srce:
010     $a  00026513
020     $a0761316035 (lib. bdg.)
040     $aDLC$cDLC$dDLC
050 00 $aPZ7.H76227$bFo 2000
082 00 $a[Fic]$221
100 1  $aHoobler, Dorothy.
245 14 $aThe 1930s :$bdirections /$cby Dorothy and Tom Hoobler.
246 30 $aDirections
260     $aBrookfield, Conn. :$bMillbrook Press,$cc2000.
300     $a159 p. :$bill. ;$c22 cm.
490 1  $aThe century kids
520     $aIn the summer of 1936, Tony runs away from his home above his
        family's Italian restaurant in Chicago, while in Berlin David is
        present at the Olympics and prepares to move to America.
611 20 $aOlympic Games$n(11th :$d1936 :$cBerlin, Germany)$vJuvenile fiction.
611 21 $aOlympic Games$n(11th :$d1936 :$cBerlin, Germany)$vFiction.
650  0 $aDepressions$y1929$vJuvenile fiction.
650  1 $aDepressions$y1929$vFiction.
650  1 $aRunaways$vFiction.
651  1 $aGermany$vFiction.
700 1  $aHoobler, Thomas.
800 1  $aHoobler, Dorothy.$tCentury kids.
```

QUIZ 4

1. What does the abbreviation OPAC stand for?

   _____

2. In an OPAC, what is a hitlist?

   _____

3. What kind of search allows us to find any word anywhere in a heading or an indexed field in a MARC record?

   [ ] Browse   [ ] Keyword

4. Do all OPAC displays look alike?

   [ ] Yes   [ ] No

5. Do all MARC displays look the same?

   [ ] Yes   [ ] No

5

MARC21 Terminology

As we have said a few times already, we used to have catalogs comprised of catalog cards, and now we have OPACs based on MARC records, but everything (and then some) that we used to put on our cards, we still put in our MARC records. Therefore, if you know the terminology from the days of catalog cards, you are not going to have any trouble with the next section of this book. However, if you don't already know this cataloging terminology, you will need to learn it here, because even though the format of our descriptions has changed a great deal (Cards→MARC), much of the terminology that we use in talking about cataloging has not.

We could just give you definitions, but as someone has said before, "a picture is worth a thousand words." Here are some pictures to illustrate what we mean by some common cataloging terms.

Note that we really don't *intend* to confuse you with the crowded illustrations that follow. We give them to you here, realizing that you might not look at them very closely to start off. However, when you get to part 2 of this book, "MARC21 Codes You Should Know," you might find it useful to return to these pages when we begin talking about the coding for a statement of responsibility or a subtitle, for example, to see what is meant by those terms. Further definitions of cataloging terms can be found in the cataloging rules should you need them (AACR 1998).

First let's look at some areas of information, as AACR calls them, starting with where they are on the title page of a book (see fig. 5.1). Then we will see how those same areas of information from the title page of the book are transcribed (entered, typed) into our catalog records.

Figure 5-2 shows descriptive areas of information on a catalog card. Remember that we provide this information in the hope that it will give patrons enough information about an item for them to decide whether or not they want to see the actual item.

Fig. 5-1 ■ Areas of Information on a Title Page

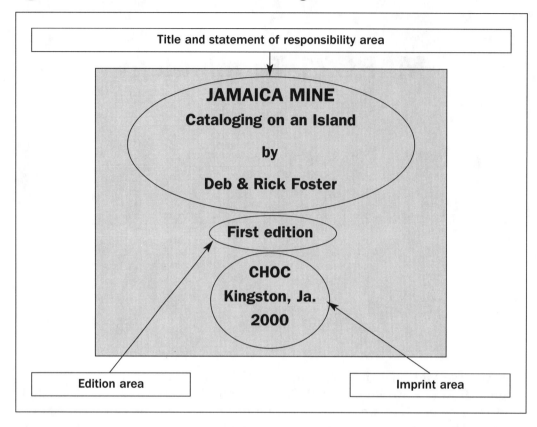

Fig. 5-2 ■ Descriptive Areas of Information on a Card

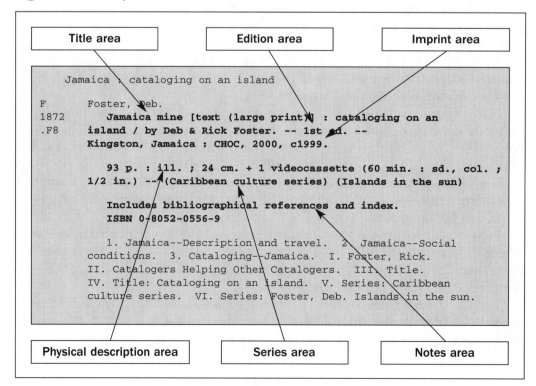

Notice that there are areas of information on the card shown in figure 5-2 that are not on the title page of the book. The information for these additional areas must have come from other places in the book.

Figure 5-3 shows how the same descriptive areas of information are entered in a MARC record.

Fig. 5-3 ■ Descriptive Areas of Information in a MARC Record

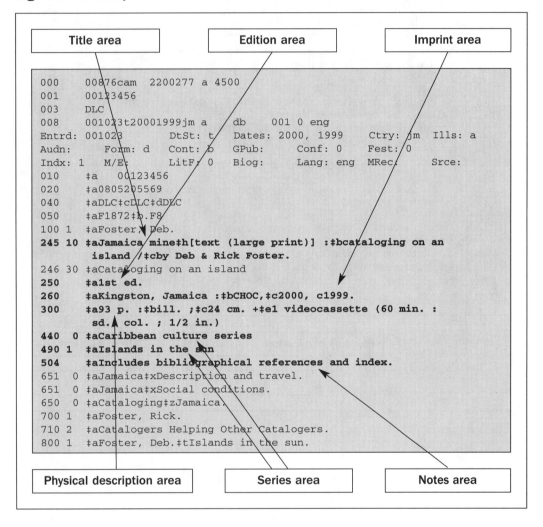

```
000     00876cam  2200277 a 4500
001     00123456
003     DLC
008     001023t20001999jm a    db    001 0 eng
Entrd: 001023        DtSt: t   Dates: 2000, 1999    Ctry: jm  Ills: a
Audn:       Form: d  Cont: b   GPub:     Conf: 0   Fest: 0
Indx: 1  M/E:        LitF: 0   Biog:     Lang: eng MRec:      Srce:
010     ‡a  00123456
020     ‡a0805205569
040     ‡aDLC‡cDLC‡dDLC
050     ‡aF1872‡b.F8
100 1   ‡aFoster, Deb.
245 10  ‡aJamaica/mine‡h[text (large print)] :‡bcataloging on an
        island /‡cby Deb & Rick Foster.
246 30  ‡aCataloging on an island
250     ‡a1st ed.
260     ‡aKingston, Jamaica :‡bCHOC,‡c2000, c1999.
300     ‡a93 p. :‡bill. ;‡c24 cm. +‡e1 videocassette (60 min. :
        sd. col. ; 1/2 in.)
440  0  ‡aCaribbean culture series
490 1   ‡aIslands in the sun
504     ‡aIncludes bibliographical references and index.
651  0  ‡aJamaica‡xDescription and travel.
651  0  ‡aJamaica‡xSocial conditions.
650  0  ‡aCataloging‡zJamaica.
700 1   ‡aFoster, Rick.
710 2   ‡aCatalogers Helping Other Catalogers.
800 1   ‡aFoster, Deb.‡tIslands in the sun.
```

Title area

Edition area

Imprint area

Physical description area

Series area

Notes area

Within the areas of information that we just outlined, we are instructed to break down the data into more specific chunks, which AACR calls elements of an area. Figure 5-4 shows elements of descriptive areas of information on a catalog card.

Fig. 5-4 ■ Elements of Descriptive Areas on a Card

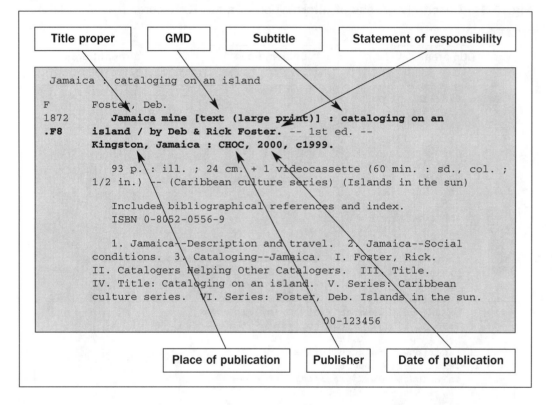

Figure 5-5 shows how the same elements of descriptive areas of information are entered in a MARC record, where they are called subfields.

Fig. 5-5 ■ Elements of Descriptive Areas in a MARC Record

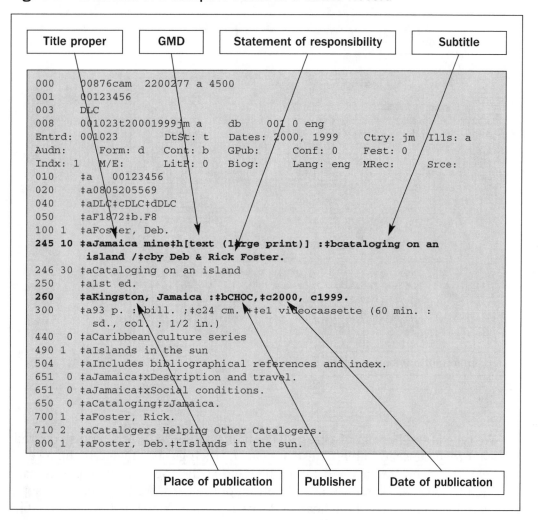

Figure 5.6 shows heading information on a card, which we provide to facilitate searching.

Fig. 5-6 ■ Headings Information on a Card

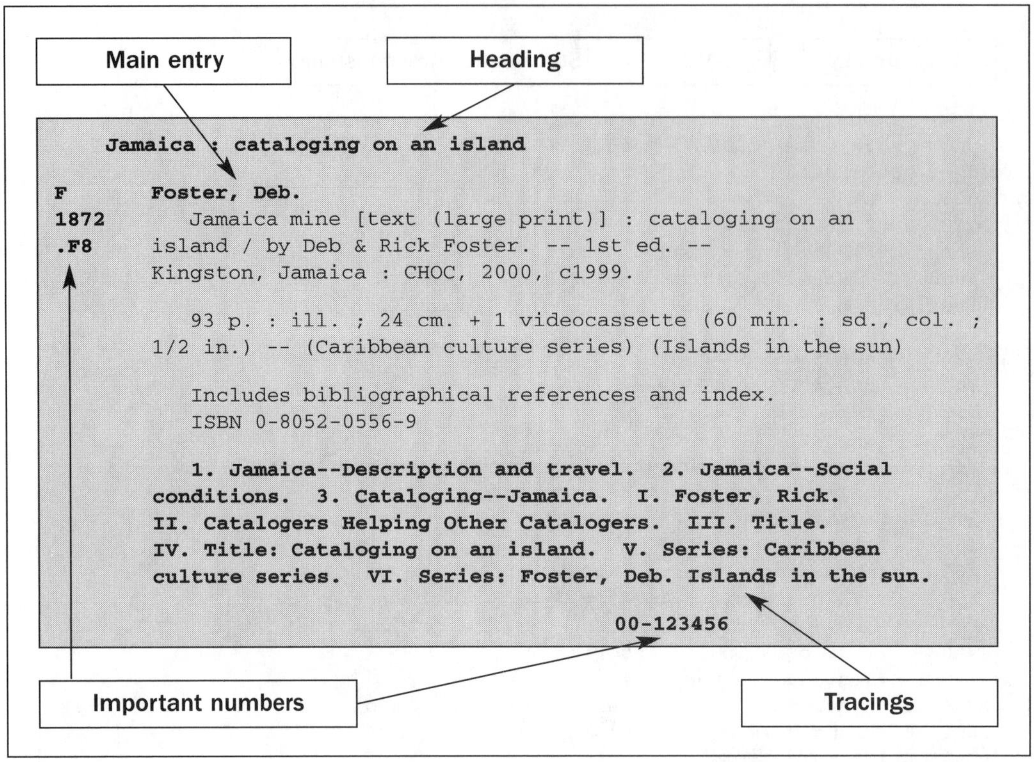

We type at the bottom of a card all the names, titles, subjects, and so on, that we want to make searchable. These are called **tracings**. Then we type up a separate card for each tracing, and type a heading at the top of each separate card for each tracing that is shown at the bottom of the card. We then file each separate card by whatever is at the head of the card, thus making headings searchable.

Figure 5-7 shows how the same headings information is entered in a MARC record. All headings fields in MARC records are indexed, and so are searchable.

Fig. 5-7 ■ Headings Information in a MARC Record

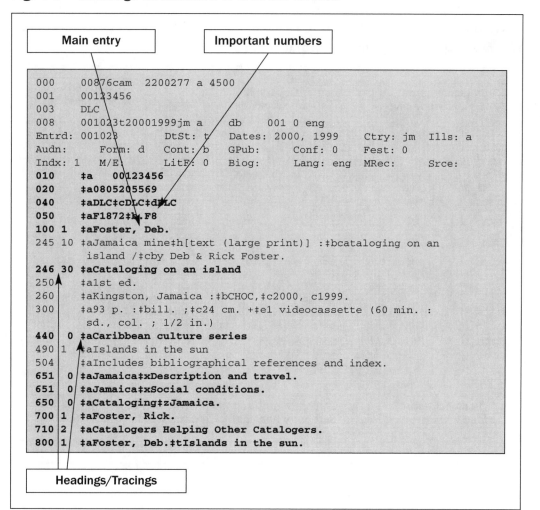

```
Main entry                    Important numbers

000      0087 6cam  2200277 a 4500
001      0012 3456
003      DLC
008      001023t20001999jm a  / db    001 0 eng
Entrd: 00102 3        DtSt: t /  Dates: 2000, 1999    Ctry: jm  Ills: a
Audn:       Form: d   Cont: /b   GPub:     Conf: 0    Fest: 0
Indx: 1    M/E        LitF: 0    Biog:     Lang: eng  MRec:      Srce:
010      ‡a   00 123456
020      ‡a0805205569
040      ‡aDLC‡cDLC‡dDLC
050      ‡aF1872‡b.F8
100 1    ‡aFoster, Deb.
245 10 ‡aJamaica mine‡h[text (large print)] :‡bcataloging on an
          island /‡cby Deb & Rick Foster.
246 30 ‡aCataloging on an island
250      ‡a1st ed.
260      ‡aKingston, Jamaica :‡bCHOC,‡c2000, c1999.
300      ‡a93 p. :‡bill. ;‡c24 cm. +‡e1 videocassette (60 min. :
          sd., col. ; 1/2 in.)
440   0  ‡aCaribbean culture series
490 1    ‡aIslands in the sun
504      ‡aIncludes bibliographical references and index.
651   0  ‡aJamaica‡xDescription and travel.
651   0  ‡aJamaica‡xSocial conditions.
650   0  ‡aCataloging‡zJamaica.
700  1   ‡aFoster, Rick.
710  2   ‡aCatalogers Helping Other Catalogers.
800  1   ‡aFoster, Deb.‡tIslands in the sun.

Headings/Tracings
```

We also have more specific terminology for headings information. For example, a main entry heading can be a personal name main entry heading (see fig. 5-7) or a corporate name main entry heading, or a conference name main entry heading.

Figure 5-8 shows some examples of specific headings information on a catalog card.

Fig. 5-8 ■ Specific Headings Information on a Card

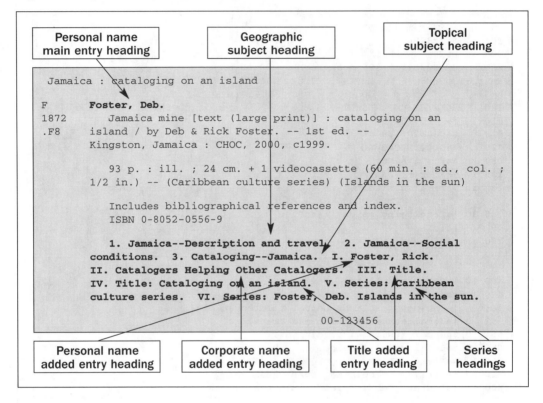

Figure 5.9 shows that the same specific headings information also appears in a MARC record.

Fig. 5-9 ■ Specific Headings Information in a MARC Record

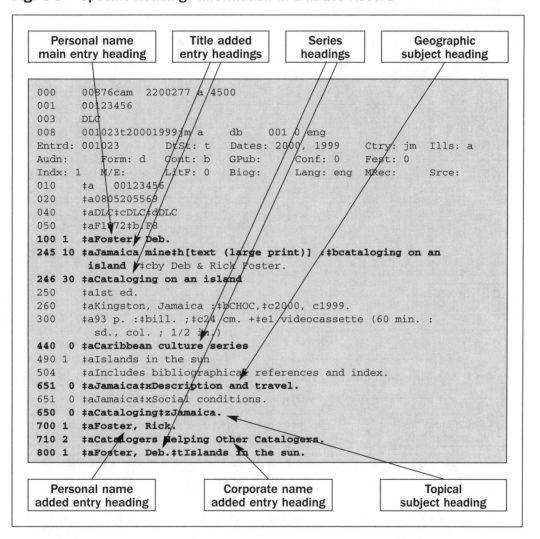

We use special punctuation, called **ISBD punctuation,** on cards to tell patrons where one type of descriptive data ends and another begins (see figs. 5-10 and 5-11). Did you know that we actually had a reason for that strange punctuation?

Fig. 5-10 ■ ISBD Punctuation on a Card

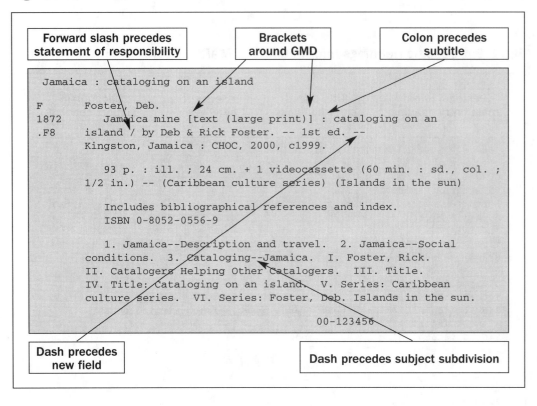

Fig. 5-11 ■ More ISBD Punctuation on a Card

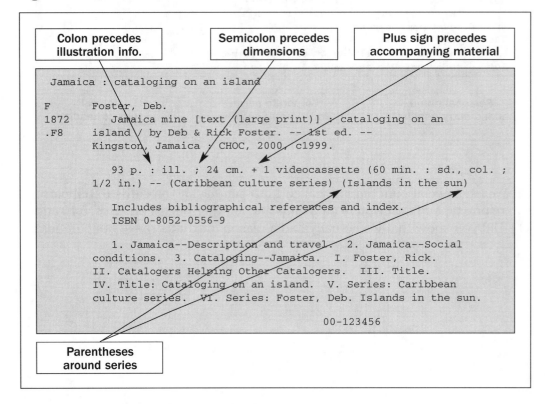

That very same punctuation is still used in MARC records (see figs. 5-12 and 5-13):

Fig. 5-12 ■ ISBD Punctuation in a MARC Record

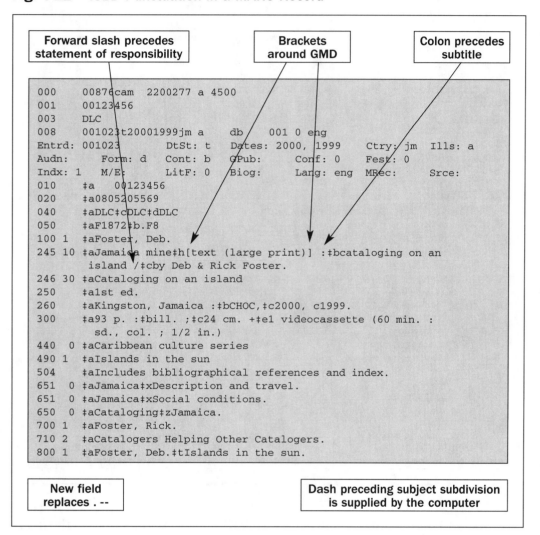

Forward slash precedes statement of responsibility

Brackets around GMD

Colon precedes subtitle

```
000     00876cam  2200277 a 4500
001     00123456
003     DLC
008     001023t20001999jm a     db    001 0 eng
Entrd: 001023          DtSt: t   Dates: 2000, 1999    Ctry: jm  Ills: a
Audn:      Form: d    Cont: b   GPub:      Conf: 0    Fest: 0
Indx: 1   M/E:        LitF: 0   Biog:      Lang: eng  MRec:      Srce:
010     ‡a  00123456
020     ‡a0805205569
040     ‡aDLC‡cDLC‡dDLC
050     ‡aF1872‡b.F8
100 1   ‡aFoster, Deb.
245 10  ‡aJamaica mine‡h[text (large print)] :‡bcataloging on an
          island /‡cby Deb & Rick Foster.
246 30  ‡aCataloging on an island
250     ‡a1st ed.
260     ‡aKingston, Jamaica :‡bCHOC,‡c2000, c1999.
300     ‡a93 p. :‡bill. ;‡c24 cm. +‡e1 videocassette (60 min. :
          sd., col. ; 1/2 in.)
440  0  ‡aCaribbean culture series
490  1  ‡aIslands in the sun
504     ‡aIncludes bibliographical references and index.
651  0  ‡aJamaica‡xDescription and travel.
651  0  ‡aJamaica‡xSocial conditions.
650  0  ‡aCataloging‡zJamaica.
700  1  ‡aFoster, Rick.
710  2  ‡aCatalogers Helping Other Catalogers.
800  1  ‡aFoster, Deb.‡tIslands in the sun.
```

New field replaces . --

Dash preceding subject subdivision is supplied by the computer

Fig. 5-13 ■ More ISBD Punctuation in a MARC Record

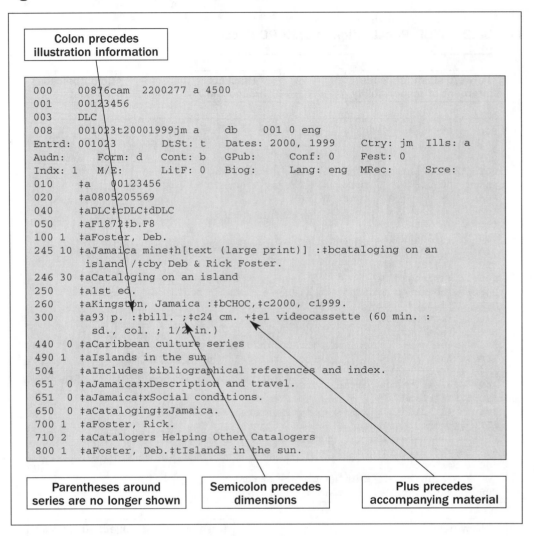

```
        Colon precedes
      illustration information

000      0087 6cam  2200277 a 4500
001      0012 3456
003      DLC
008      001023t20001999jm a    db    001 0 eng
Entrd: 001023        DtSt: t    Dates: 2000, 1999    Ctry: jm  Ills: a
Audn:      Form: d   Cont: b   GPub:      Conf: 0    Fest: 0
Indx: 1    M/E:      LitF: 0   Biog:      Lang: eng  MRec:      Srce:
010      ‡a   00123456
020      ‡a0805205569
040      ‡aDLC‡cDLC‡dDLC
050      ‡aF1872‡b.F8
100 1    ‡aFoster, Deb.
245 10   ‡aJamaica mine‡h[text (large print)] :‡bcataloging on an
           island /‡cby Deb & Rick Foster.
246 30   ‡aCataloging on an island
250      ‡a1st ed.
260      ‡aKingston, Jamaica :‡bCHOC,‡c2000, c1999.
300      ‡a93 p. :‡bill. ;‡c24 cm. +‡e1 videocassette (60 min. :
           sd., col. ; 1/2 in.)
440  0   ‡aCaribbean culture series
490 1    ‡aIslands in the sun
504      ‡aIncludes bibliographical references and index.
651  0   ‡aJamaica‡xDescription and travel.
651  0   ‡aJamaica‡xSocial conditions.
650  0   ‡aCataloging‡zJamaica.
700 1    ‡aFoster, Rick.
710 2    ‡aCatalogers Helping Other Catalogers
800 1    ‡aFoster, Deb.‡tIslands in the sun.
```

| Parentheses around series are no longer shown | Semicolon precedes dimensions | Plus precedes accompanying material |

This ISBD punctuation displays in the OPAC to help patrons to read the fields more clearly (see figs. 5-14 and 5-15).

Fig. 5-14 ■ ISBD Punctuation in the OPAC

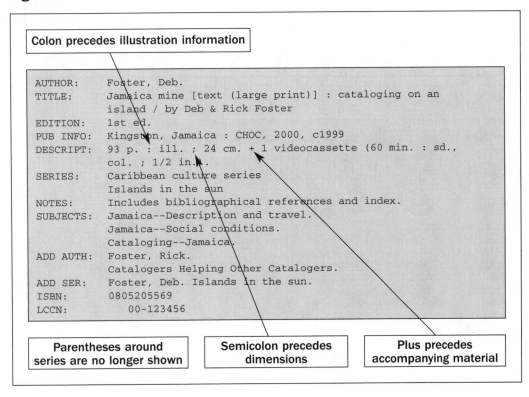

Forward slash precedes statement of responsibility

Brackets around GMD

Colon precedes subtitle

```
AUTHOR:    Foster, Deb.
TITLE:     Jamaica mine [text (large print)] : cataloging on an
           island / by Deb & Rick Foster
EDITION:   1st ed.
PUB INFO:  Kingston, Jamaica : CHOC, 2000, c1999
DESCRIPT:  93 p. : ill. ; 24 cm. + 1 videocassette (60 min. : sd.,
           col. ; 1/2 in.).
SERIES:    Caribbean culture series
           Islands in the sun
NOTES:     Includes bibliographical references and index.
SUBJECTS:  Jamaica--Description and travel.
           Jamaica--Social conditions.
           Cataloging--Jamaica.
ADD AUTH:  Foster, Rick.
           Catalogers Helping Other Catalogers.
ADD SER:   Foster, Deb. Islands in the sun.
ISBN:      0805205569
LCCN:        00-123456
```

Dash precedes subject subdivision

Fig. 5-15 ■ More ISBD Punctuation in the OPAC

Colon precedes illustration information

```
AUTHOR:    Foster, Deb.
TITLE:     Jamaica mine [text (large print)] : cataloging on an
           island / by Deb & Rick Foster
EDITION:   1st ed.
PUB INFO:  Kingston, Jamaica : CHOC, 2000, c1999
DESCRIPT:  93 p. : ill. ; 24 cm. + 1 videocassette (60 min. : sd.,
           col. ; 1/2 in.).
SERIES:    Caribbean culture series
           Islands in the sun
NOTES:     Includes bibliographical references and index.
SUBJECTS:  Jamaica--Description and travel.
           Jamaica--Social conditions.
           Cataloging--Jamaica.
ADD AUTH:  Foster, Rick.
           Catalogers Helping Other Catalogers.
ADD SER:   Foster, Deb. Islands in the sun.
ISBN:      0805205569
LCCN:        00-123456
```

Parentheses around series are no longer shown

Semicolon precedes dimensions

Plus precedes accompanying material

Special MARC Terms

The preceding pages told you about terms that have been carried over into the MARC world from the card days. However, there are also some new terms that you need to learn.

A MARC Tag and Field

A MARC **tag** is a three-digit number that identifies the kind of data that will be found in the field associated with it. For example, in the MARC21 bibliographic format, *title information* will be found in the field associated with tag 245 (see fig. 5-16).

> **MARCspeak**
> There is a special way of saying tag numbers. For example:
>
> for tag 245, say "two-forty-five," not "two hundred and forty-five";
>
> for tag 010, say "oh-one-oh," not "ten";
>
> for tag 008, say oh-oh-eight," not "eight" and not "zero-zero-eight."
>
> for tag 600, say "six hundred," not "six-oh-oh";

Fig. 5-16 ■ A Tag and Field in a MARC Record

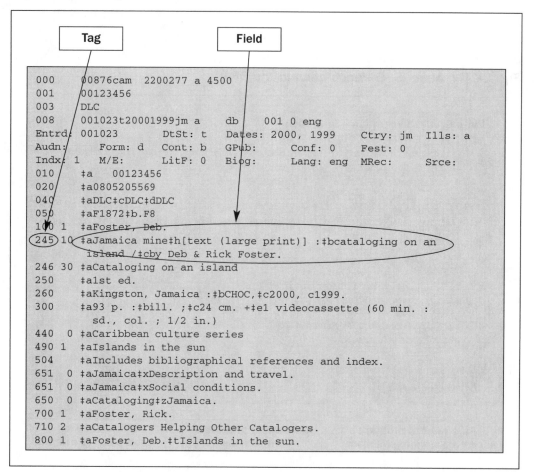

for tag 650, say "six fifty," not "six hundred and fifty," or "six-five-oh."

The term *6XX* means any tag beginning with 6, e.g., 600, 610, 611, 630, 650, 651, 655, 690, 691; *4XX* means any tag beginning with 4, e.g., 440, 490, etc.

A MARC **field** is the entire string of information identified by the tag, e.g., the complete title and other information in the 245 tag. The data in fields is further broken down into subfields (more on this later). Some fields are **repeatable,** some are not.

MARCspeak

Say "245 field" when you mean the actual data, and say "245 tag" when you mean the numbers.

MARC Indicators

A MARC *indicator* is a one-digit code (either a number or a blank space) that gives the system special instructions about the data found in the field that follows it (see fig. 5-17). Some **indicator values** are there to instruct the system on

Fig. 5-17 ■ Indicators in a MARC Record

```
Two indicators

000     00876cam  2200277 a 4500
001     00123456
003     DLC
008     001023t20001999jm a     db     001 0 eng
Entrd:  001023      DtSt: t    Dates: 2000, 1999    Ctry: jm  Ills: a
Audn:       Form: d  Cont: b   GPub:      Conf: 0   Fest: 0
Indx: 1   M/E:       LitF: 0   Biog:      Lang: eng MRec:     Srce:
010     ‡a   00123456
020     ‡a0805205569
040     ‡aDLC‡cDLC‡dDLC
050     ‡aF1872‡b.F8
100 1   ‡aFoster, Deb.
245 10  ‡aJamaica mine‡h[text (large print)] :‡bcataloging on an
        island /‡cby Deb & Rick Foster.
246 30  ‡aCataloging on an island
250     ‡a1st ed.
260     ‡aKingston, Jamaica :‡bCHOC,‡c2000, c1999.
300     ‡a93 p. :‡bill. ;‡c24 cm. +‡e1 videocassette (60 min. :
        sd., col. ; 1/2 in.)
440  0  ‡aCaribbean culture series
490  1  ‡aIslands in the sun
504     ‡aIncludes bibliographical references and index.
651  0  ‡aJamaica‡xDescription and travel.
651  0  ‡aJamaica‡xSocial conditions.
650  0  ‡aCataloging‡zJamaica.
700  1  ‡aFoster, Rick.
710  2  ‡aCatalogers Helping Other Catalogers.
800  1  ‡aFoster, Deb.‡tIslands in the sun.
```

how to file the data in the field; others tell the system whether to index or display the field or both, and still others tell the system when to provide special labels (called **display constants**) when displaying the field in an OPAC.

All fields have **indicator positions** except the control fields (000–008). It is important (though confusing) to note that a blank space is a valid indicator value. Sometimes it will mean nothing (e.g., 010 first and second indicators), and sometimes it will mean something (e.g., 700 second indicator). See chapters 7 and 10 for the meanings of the indicators in these two examples.

MARCspeak

> Refer to indicators as "first indicator" and "second indicator," or "indicator one" and "indicator two," or "I1" and "I2."
>
> Always say tag + indicator, e.g., "245 indicator one," not just "indicator one," because indicators have different meanings in different tags.
>
> Do not say "245 indicators are ten"; say "245 indicator one is one and indicator two is zero."

A MARC Subfield Delimiter and Subfield Code

A MARC **subfield delimiter** is a special character that tells the system that what follows it is a subfield code and is not part of the cataloging information in the field (see fig. 5-18). These subfield delimiters display differently in different systems (e.g., OCLC: ‡, ITS: ▼, Athena: $), but they are always the same special character in the raw MARC record (ASCII 031).

A MARC **subfield code** is an alphanumeric code (0–9 or a–z) that identifies the kind of data that will be found in the subfield that follows it (see fig. 5-18). For example, the subfield code b in the 260 field indicates that publisher data will be found there. On the other hand, a subfield code b in the 300 field indicates that additional physical description information will be found there. Subfield codes have different meanings in different tags, just like indicators.

MARCspeak

> Some people say "delimiter b" to refer to a subfield, some say "subfield b," and some say "dollar b." They all mean the same thing.

Fig. 5-18 ■ A Subfield Delimiter and Subfield Code in a MARC Record

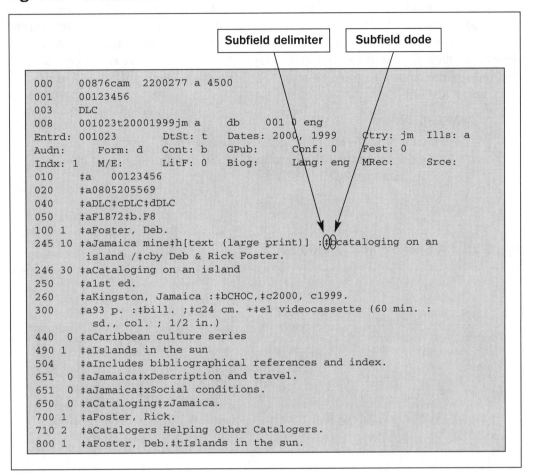

```
000      00876cam  2200277 a 4500
001      00123456
003      DLC
008      001023t20001999jm a     db    001 0 eng
Entrd: 001023      DtSt: t   Dates: 2000, 1999   Ctry: jm  Ills: a
Audn:       Form: d  Cont: b   GPub:       Conf: 0   Fest: 0
Indx: 1   M/E:      LitF: 0   Biog:       Lang: eng  MRec:      Srce:
010      ‡a   00123456
020      ‡a0805205569
040      ‡aDLC‡cDLC‡dDLC
050      ‡aF1872‡b.F8
100 1    ‡aFoster, Deb.
245 10   ‡aJamaica mine‡h[text (large print)] :‡bcataloging on an
           island /‡cby Deb & Rick Foster.
246 30   ‡aCataloging on an island
250      ‡a1st ed.
260      ‡aKingston, Jamaica :‡bCHOC,‡c2000, c1999.
300      ‡a93 p. :‡bill. ;‡c24 cm. +‡e1 videocassette (60 min. :
           sd., col. ; 1/2 in.)
440  0   ‡aCaribbean culture series
490 1    ‡aIslands in the sun
504      ‡aIncludes bibliographical references and index.
651  0   ‡aJamaica‡xDescription and travel.
651  0   ‡aJamaica‡xSocial conditions.
650  0   ‡aCataloging‡zJamaica.
700 1    ‡aFoster, Rick.
710 2    ‡aCatalogers Helping Other Catalogers.
800 1    ‡aFoster, Deb.‡tIslands in the sun.
```

Subfield delimiter

Subfield dode

A MARC Subfield

A MARC **subfield** is the string of information identified by the subfield code (see fig. 5-19). Breaking the field into smaller chunks allows us to give the system more precise instructions about *which* data will be indexed and displayed and *how* those data will be indexed and displayed. Some fields have only one subfield defined for them; others have as many as thirty-five. Some subfields are repeatable, some are not.

> **MARCspeak**
>
> Always say tag + subfield, e.g., "245 subfield c," not just "subfield c," because the data in a 245$c is quite different from the data in a 260$c.

Fig. 5-19 ■ A Subfield in a MARC Record

MARC Control Fields Data

These special fields are called *control fields* by LC and fixed fields by OCLC. MARC **control fields** data (see fig. 5-20) is coded information that is used by the system to quickly identify what the record is about (000) and to provide search qualifiers (008), both of which we will talk about, in chapter 9, "Coded Fields." Fixed fields are not repeatable.

MARCspeak

Usually, if you say "fixed field," you mean the 000 and the 008 combined, as OCLC shows them. Most non-OCLC people refer to them separately.

When referring to the 000, say "oh-oh-oh," not "zero-zero-zero." Some people find it much easier to call it the "leader," however.

Fig. 5-20 ■ MARC Control Fields Data

```
                        ┌─────────────────────┐
                        │  Control fields data │
                        └─────────────────────┘

 000      00876cam  2200277 a 4500
 001      00123456
 003      DLC
 008      001023t20001999jm a      db    001 0 eng
 Entrd: 001023      DtSt: t   Dates: 2000, 1999    Ctry: jm  Ills: a
 Audn:      Form: d  Cont: b   GPub:      Conf: 0   Fest: 0
 Indx: 1    M/E:     LitF: 0   Biog:     Lang: eng MRec:    Srce:
 010      ‡a   00123456
 020      ‡a0805205569
 040      ‡aDLC‡cDLC‡dDLC
 050      ‡aF1872‡b.F8
 100 1    ‡aFoster, Deb.
 245 10   ‡aJamaica mine‡h[text (large print)] :‡bcataloging on an
             island /‡cby Deb & Rick Foster.
 246 30   ‡aCataloging on an island
 250      ‡a1st ed.
 260      ‡aKingston, Jamaica :‡bCHOC,‡c2000, c1999.
 300      ‡a93 p. :‡bill. ;‡c24 cm. +‡e1 videocassette (60 min. :
             sd., col. ; 1/2 in.)
 440   0  ‡aCaribbean culture series
 490 1    ‡aIslands in the sun
 504      ‡aIncludes bibliographical references and index.
 651   0  ‡aJamaica‡xDescription and travel.
 651   0  ‡aJamaica‡xSocial conditions.
 650   0  ‡aCataloging‡zJamaica.
 700 1    ‡aFoster, Rick.
 710 2    ‡aCatalogers Helping Other Catalogers.
 800 1    ‡aFoster, Deb.‡tIslands in the sun.
```

QUIZ 5

Connect the following terms to the MARC record

The leader   A tag   An indicator   A field   A subfield delimiter

```
000      00876cam  2200277 a 4500
001      00123456
003      DLC
008      001023t20001999jm a     db    001 0 eng
Entrd: 001023          DtSt: t   Dates: 2000, 1999      Ctry: jm  Ills: a
Audn:       Form: d   Cont: b   GPub:       Conf: 0   Fest: 0
Indx: 1   M/E:      LitF: 0   Biog:       Lang: eng  MRec:      Srce:
010      ‡a   00123456
020      ‡a0805205569
040      ‡aDLC‡cDLC‡dDLC
050      ‡aF1872‡b.F8
100  1   ‡aFoster, Deb.
245  10  ‡aJamaica mine‡h[text (large print)] :‡bcataloging on an
           island /‡cby Deb & Rick Foster.
246  30  ‡aCataloging on an island
250      ‡a1st ed.
260      ‡aKingston, Jamaica :‡bCHOC,‡c2000, c1999.
300      ‡a93 p. :‡bill. ;‡c24 cm. +‡e1 videocassette (60 min. :
           sd., col. ; 1/2 in.)
440   0  ‡aCaribbean culture series
490  1   ‡aIslands in the sun
504      ‡aIncludes bibliographical references and index.
651   0  ‡aJamaica‡xDescription and travel.
651   0  ‡aJamaica‡xSocial conditions.
650   0  ‡aCataloging‡zJamaica.
700  1   ‡aFoster, Rick.
710  2   ‡aCatalogers Helping Other Catalogers.
800  1   ‡aFoster, Deb.‡tIslands in the sun.
```

Edition area   A note field   Statement of responsibility   A subfield code

6

MARC21—Who Needs to Know What

If you are not a cataloger, you will not need to know everything about MARC, and, no doubt, you will not want to either! But depending upon which part of the library you happen to work in, your reasons for knowing a bit about MARC will vary. We would like to take a few moments to emphasize which aspects of MARC might most interest which particular groups of library staff, and why. We will introduce a few concepts or phrases that we won't explain until the following chapter, but we think it is important to paint this "who needs to know what" picture before we go any farther.

Acquisitions Staff

Until fairly recently, acquisitions people did not need to know anything about MARC. They manually gathered requests for materials, typed the order information for those requests on forms or entered it into a computer, sent in the orders, and possibly created lists of **on-order** materials. In the card catalog environment, acquisitions staff often placed order slips in the **shelflist catalog** (a catalog arranged by call number, i.e., in the same order as the items were arranged on the shelves, ergo, "shelflist"), so that other staffers could know about items that would soon be available.

In an OPAC environment, MARC records for on-order materials have replaced order slips in many libraries. In some systems these records are visible to the patrons; in others, they are visible only to the staff. In some cases, patrons can even put **holds** on those materials in anticipation of their arrival and processing.

In the early days, the on-order records that acquisitions people made were very simple, minimal MARC records (or, in some cases, not MARC records at all), with just enough information to be searched by an author's name and a title. As access to MARC records improved, it became apparent that the time needed to create a minimal MARC record was not much less than the time needed to find a complete MARC record (whenever possible) for on-order material.

Now, just like copy catalogers, acquisitions people have to go to the library's source of MARC records and attempt to find records that accurately match the items that are on order. This can be somewhat challenging, because acquisitions people often are not given as much training as copy catalogers, and so do not know very much about the intricacies of matching records: to ensure that every field in the record that is downloaded truly matches the material that is going to be purchased.

This brings us to another interesting dilemma for acquisitions people: they do not actually have the material to look at when they are looking for MARC records (catalogers call this "having the item in-hand"). It is therefore that much harder for acquisitions people to find the correct MARC record for the material in question. Lack of training plus this lack of the actual items in-hand means that all on-order records must be carefully checked against the actual items once they are in-hand, because it may turn out that the downloaded records will not quite match the actual items.

Because the whole purpose of an on-order MARC record is to provide patrons and staff with the same detailed descriptions and access for on-order materials as for materials already in the collection, it seems logical that acquisitions people should be given the same training as copy catalogers. Acquisitions people must be able to read MARC records and must be familiar with the appropriate **match criteria** for the materials that they handle.[1]

The MARC fields that will matter most to acquisitions staff, therefore, are those that affect record matching (number fields) and those that contain the description of an item (display fields).

Circulation Staff

Circulation people do not often see MARC records unless they run into something that doesn't make sense. When they do encounter problems, they should at least know enough about MARC to understand that the computer is not acting up or being whimsical.

It is even possible that knowing a little about MARC might help circulation staff explain certain system issues to patrons. Consider the following scenario: a patron places a hold on a book and grows weary of waiting for notification that the book is available, so he asks the most visible staff member in the library—a circulation person—what the holdup might be. It turns out there are three records in the system for the book: one for a large-print edition, one for a regular-print, illustrated edition published by Grossett and Dunlap, and one for a regular-print edition published by Knopf with an important introduction. The patron placed a hold on the large-print edition because it was the first book that displayed in the hitlist. Every other patron who wanted that book did the same thing! Thus, even though the two regular-print books are patiently waiting on the shelf, our patron still has a few months to wait before his name gets to the top of the list—waiting for the much-requested large-print edition to make the rounds!

Despite popular, uninformed opinion, the solution for this particular problem is *not* to use one MARC record for these three different publications. Some patrons really do want to borrow only large print; others might be specifically looking for the introduction in the Knopf edition. The system should be able to allow holds to be placed across all records for a given work, as well as specially placed on a particular record. If the system cannot do this, then circulation staff should be able to explain to patrons why the library has multiple records for different editions of a work, and, if necessary, help them to switch their holds to less-popular records. Understanding the need for accurate bibliographic information and learning how to look at MARC records can help circulation staff see the finer distinctions between records, which might not be as obvious in the OPAC displays.

Here's another example of how knowing a bit about MARC records could help circulation people. As we shall see in chapter 10 when we get to *machine matching,* sometimes barcode numbers get attached to the wrong records, which will make it look as though a patron has borrowed something she didn't. Circulation people need to know that this can happen and why, and when it does happen they should be able to find the affected MARC record and report it to cataloging so that the problem can be fixed.

The MARC fields that will matter most to circulation staff, therefore, are those that affect record matching (number fields) and those that contain the description of an item (display fields).

ILL Staff

Once upon a time, interlibrary loan (ILL) was a time-consuming and laborious task. If a library was so fortunate as to have a copy of the NUC (National Union Catalog), it was possible to find out what materials were held by the largest libraries in the United States and Canada and then fill out a paper form to request that the owning institution loan the material. If the library did not have access to the NUC, then that same request could be sent blind to a central site (often a state library) in the hope that the central site could find a library that did have the material.

These days, in some libraries, patrons can make ILL requests directly from the OCLC union catalog (by using their online catalog as a gateway to OCLC's FirstSearch) or from their virtual union catalogs. Most often, however, patron-originated requests for out-of-library materials are forwarded to library staff for approval. ILL people will be able to do a much better job of selecting exactly the right records to use for requesting materials if they are able to read MARC records and distinguish the sometimes subtle differences between seemingly identical titles.

The MARC fields that will matter most to ILL staff are those that affect record matching (number fields) and those that contain the descriptions of the items (display fields) to be sure that staff are requesting the correct material.

Reference Staff

Reference people may be interested in learning why some searches fail and why the records display for patrons the way they do. They should know something about the fields that affect how patrons can search (indexed fields and coded fields) and what they will see (display fields). Reference people also often have to answer questions about holds and ILL and so should know at least as much as circulation and ILL people about MARC.

Many libraries insist that catalogers spend some time on the reference desk. The idea is that if catalogers see how patrons actually use the catalog, it will improve their view of the "big picture" of the library and help them to create more relevant access points in their MARC records.

We think the reverse should also be true. Even though most reference librarians could not do cataloging for love or money, they should at least be more familiar with what catalogers do, and that especially includes understanding MARC, because MARC is fundamental to the construction of the catalog. As one reference librarian (John Iliff) put it, "Each and every one of those [MARC] records represents, when done properly, a consistent intellectual exercise in helping to pinpoint needles in haystacks—which is all a reference librarian does."

Administrative Staff

Directors need to know how everything fits together to make a workable library catalog. It is imperative that directors understand that not all MARC records are equal, and that a good MARC record is going to do a much better job in an automation system than a bad MARC record. They also need to know that a good MARC record that does not quite match the item that it is supposed to be describing is even worse than a bad MARC record because it gives misleading information, frustrating both staff and patrons.

It is an awe-inspiring thought (and one that we have often discussed between ourselves) that someday every item that is published will have a truly unique identifier and will be cataloged once and only once by some Great Cataloging Factory that will place the unique identifier in a single perfect MARC record. From that moment on, every library that purchases that item can use that unique identifier to access that one perfect MARC record and download that record to its database.

This is how most directors perceive that cataloging already works in their libraries. To some degree we are slowly approaching this goal, because of cataloging-sharing agencies like OCLC and RLIN, and other means of access to records from LC and other libraries. Unfortunately, however, we do not yet have a truly unique identifier to make copy cataloging simple, nor are all materials yet cataloged perfectly by someone else. Regrettably, it is often the materials that are most valuable to patrons that do not fit into this highly automated and streamlined process. So, directors, until that glorious day of quick, easy, and perfect cataloging arrives, your staff members still need to know enough about MARC to be sure that the records they are getting from whatever source(s) truly match their items. They may even have to know how to make their own MARC records from scratch.

Most directors have some idea of how to handle a reference question or circulate an item in a pinch, so it only seems reasonable that they should at least know enough about MARC and how it works that they can wisely advise their staff, "garbage in, garbage out." It even seems a good business investment to make the commitment to catalog correctly from the start, since the library catalog will be providing access to the library collection long after any particular individuals involved in the process have departed.

Catalogers

The long and the short of it is that catalogers need to know everything about MARC, in much more detail than we will cover here.

Remember that before we had MARC, long, long ago, every cataloger had to catalog every item from scratch, typing multiple catalog cards, then filing them in the card catalog. Even just making a typo was a horrible experience, because, if the supervisor was strict, the cataloger could not erase the mistake, but had to completely redo the card.

Of all people in the library, catalogers should love MARC most, because it has revolutionized the most mundane part of their work—typing and filing multiple cards—while preserving the best part of it—the intellectual activity involved in describing library materials and providing access to these materials in the online catalog.

Catalogers must know the descriptive cataloging rules; they must know how to assign subject headings and classification numbers; they must know how to be sure that they are copying the correct records. When they cannot find a MARC record that exactly matches the item that they have in-hand, they must know how to use a similar record to make a new one that does exactly match the item. When they cannot find anything close, they must know how to make an original record from scratch.

Catalogers should also start to think about MARC records not only individually but also as a collection—a database. Catalogers should know how their systems identify duplicate records, index MARC records, display them, and so on, as well as how coding affects all these functions. That is a great deal to know, and this book is not going to begin to cover it all. Try *Cataloging with AACR2R and USMARC* (Fritz 1999) for many more details on cataloging rules and MARC coding, and for cheatsheets that may help you to learn how to copy and create good MARC records.

Systems Staff

Last, but not at all least, the person responsible for running a library's system needs to know almost all the things that we have just said the cataloger needs to know. Nothing is so disheartening in a library as a systems person who has no knowledge at all of MARC. In such an unfortunate situation, the automated system often ends up taking on a separate existence, divorced from its reason for being (the library's catalog), cloaked in technobabble that is meaningless to everyone else in the library. A little knowledge of MARC will go a long way to help the systems people to bridge this communications gap.

The plain fact of the matter is that most, if not all, library automation systems run on MARC records. It is that simple. Although systems staff members may not need to know as much about MARC as the catalogers, the more MARC they do know, the more valuable they will be to their library.

Loading MARC records creates the database for the system. Systems staff members need to know how their systems load MARC records, and how their systems react when two records seem to be the same. This means that they need to know how the number fields in the MARC record work.

Indexing the MARC records creates the online catalog, and this means that systems staff need to know about the headings fields: which ones are indexed and where, and how to change this, if requested by the catalogers.

Finally, the OPAC displays that the patrons see are created as the system extracts and formats data from the MARC record. Systems staff need to know about the display fields in the records, which ones display where, and how to change this, if requested by the catalogers.[2]

If you are a systems person, you should find MARC surprisingly easy to learn, compared to the inner workings of many library systems that we have seen. We know that you have a million fires to put out, and that often your lunch consists of gulping down a peanut butter sandwich as you hammer out computer instructions on your keyboard. But we promise you that, rather than making your job harder, acquiring a working knowledge of MARC will actually make it easier. Many hitherto mysterious details will suddenly become amazingly clear once you gain a solid knowledge of MARC. You will be able to perform herculean tasks and amaze your colleagues with miraculous works. Again, as for catalogers, this book will not teach you everything you need to know about MARC, but it will definitely give you a good foundation upon which to build.[3]

QUIZ 6

1. Which MARC fields will matter most to circulation, acquisitions, and ILL people?

_____

2. Which MARC fields will matter most to reference people?

_____

3. Which MARC fields will matter most to catalogers and systems people?

_____

4. What is the least that directors should know about MARC?

_____

Notes

1. You will find details on match criteria in the OCLC *Bibliographic Formats and Standards Manual* (OCLC 1993) or in my earlier book, *Cataloging with AACR2R and USMARC* (ALA 1999).

2. Although changes to OPAC displays are often requested by public services staff, our contention is that catalogers should coordinate any change to the catalog, including changes to the display. In the absence of any kind of OPAC standard, keeping the catalogers in charge of the catalog is the best way to ensure consistency between your catalog and the catalogs of others.

3. Systems people should definitely read Walt Crawford's *MARC for Library Use* (1989). Though somewhat old for a technical work, it is still the best introduction to MARC for library systems staff and programmers.

## PART II

MARC21 Codes You Should Know

We are about to begin looking at a great many examples of MARC fields, and we want to begin with the reminder that we are not going to mention every possible MARC field or subfield code that exists. In other words, please do *not* try to use this book as a MARC coding manual.

Our approach is to present you with the most common fields found in MARC21 bibliographic records, and introduce you to some of the main patterns and symmetries in the coding, so that you will be able to read MARC records with relative ease.

If, and when, you are ready for a more comprehensive treatment of MARC coding, you will find that information readily available from other sources, especially the Library of Congress MARC website (*MARC21 Concise* 1999), which is available on the Internet and is the definitive—and most current—source of documentation on MARC coding.

Field Groups

We are going to take the universe of MARC fields and divide it into four general groups, thinking most particularly about how the coding in those fields affects what patrons can see and what they can search:

> *Indexed fields,* specifically the fields that contain the headings or access points that are used for searching.
>
> *Display fields,* in particular the most common fields that are used to describe library materials, i.e., that contain our bibliographic descriptions.

Coded fields, particularly the fields that are useful for qualifying or limiting searches. By *coded* we mean that the data in these fields comes from various lists of possible values or codes.

Number fields, primarily the fields that contain numbers, such as LCCN or ISBN, that are used for searching and are intended to uniquely identify records in a database.

If you are interested, see appendix B for a complete list of every possible MARC field (assigned as of late 2001).

Important: In all the MARC tables in the chapters following, we list only the most common indicators and subfields for each field.[1]

Note

1. For a complete list of MARC data elements for each field, please consult a MARC manual or go to the MARC21 manual at the Library of Congress MARC home page on the Internet (*MARC21 Concise* 1999).

7

Indexed Fields—Headings

Names, titles, and subjects are all considered headings, something that a patron might want to search by. They are sometimes called *access points* for the same reason. As we mentioned earlier, the term *heading* probably comes from the fact that the name, title, or subject was typed at the top, or head, of a catalog card, and the card was then filed alphabetically by that name, title, or subject, thus making the heading searchable.

The concept of main entry versus added entries might seem outdated to some, but we still have to deal with it, because it has been carried over into the MARC world and influences our coding there.

A **main entry** is a heading for a person, **corporate body,** or conference that we have deemed to be solely or primarily responsible for the intellectual and/or artistic content of a work. A **uniform title** can also be a main entry (per the very specific set of rules provided in AACR2).

Added entries, on the other hand, are headings that we include for people, corporate bodies, conferences, or titles that are not the main entry but are somehow related to a work.

In figure 7-1, the heading "Foster, Deb" is given at the head of the card as the main entry for this book. The added entries are given at the bottom of the card, and for them to be searchable, a separate card would have to be made with each added entry at the head of the card, above the main entry (see also fig. 5-2).

Fig. 7-1 ■ Main and Added Entries on a Card

Main entry

```
F        Foster, Deb.
1872        Jamaica mine [text (large print)] : cataloging on
.F8      an island / by Deb & Rick Foster. -- 1st
         ed. -- Kingston, Jamaica : CHOC, 2000, c1999.

            93 p. : ill. ; 24 cm. + 1 videocassette (60 min. :
         sd., col. ; 1/2 in.) -- (Caribbean culture series)
         (Islands in the sun)

            Includes bibliographical references and index.
            ISBN 0-8052-0556-9

            1. Jamaica--Description and travel.  2. Jamaica--
         Social conditions.  3. Cataloging--Jamaica.  I. Foster,
         Rick.  II. Catalogers Helping Other Catalogers.  III.
         Title.  IV. Title: Cataloging on an island.  V. Series:
         Caribbean culture series.  VI. Series: Foster, Deb.
         Islands in the sun.

                                            00-123456
```

Added entries

MARC Tags for Headings

Headings (names, titles, and subjects) are divided in MARC according to what each heading refers to. For example, is a particular name the name of a person, a corporation, or a conference? Does a given **subject heading** refer to a thing (topical) or to a place (geographic)? Is that title the actual name of the item, or is it a term that has been standardized by the cataloger (a uniform title)? These distinctions determine both the appropriate cataloging rules and the MARC coding that applies to those headings.

Using the chart in figure 7-2, we can deduce that:

- the main entry for a personal name is coded 100 in MARC (because main entry tags always begin with 1 and personal name tags always end in 00);

- a subject heading for a meeting or conference is coded 611 in MARC (because subject tags always begin with 6, and conference name tags always end in 11);

- an added entry for a corporate name is coded 710 in MARC (because added entry tags always begin with 7 and corporate name tags always end in 10).

See how easy it is to learn MARC coding (for headings at any rate)!

In the online catalog, these headings are usually indexed according to three main groups or contexts: name indexes, title indexes, and subject indexes.

Name indexes are created from the following headings and MARC fields:

personal names (100, 700, 800)

corporate names (110, 710, 810)

conference names (111, 711, 811)

Fig. 7-2 ■ Patterns in MARC Headings Tags

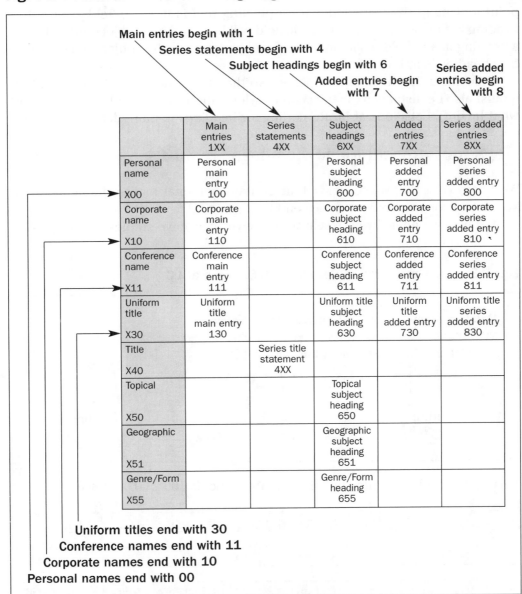

	Main entries 1XX	Series statements 4XX	Subject headings 6XX	Added entries 7XX	Series added entries 8XX
Personal name X00	Personal main entry 100		Personal subject heading 600	Personal added entry 700	Personal series added entry 800
Corporate name X10	Corporate main entry 110		Corporate subject heading 610	Corporate added entry 710	Corporate series added entry 810
Conference name X11	Conference main entry 111		Conference subject heading 611	Conference added entry 711	Conference series added entry 811
Uniform title X30	Uniform title main entry 130		Uniform title subject heading 630	Uniform title added entry 730	Uniform title series added entry 830
Title X40		Series title statement 4XX			
Topical X50			Topical subject heading 650		
Geographic X51			Geographic subject heading 651		
Genre/Form X55			Genre/Form heading 655		

Main entries begin with 1
Series statements begin with 4
Subject headings begin with 6
Added entries begin with 7
Series added entries begin with 8

Uniform titles end with 30
Conference names end with 11
Corporate names end with 10
Personal names end with 00

Subject indexes are created from the following headings and MARC fields:

> personal names as subjects (600)
>
> corporate names as subjects (610)
>
> conference names as subjects (611)
>
> uniform titles as subjects (630)
>
> subject headings (650, 651, 655)

Title indexes are created from the following headings and MARC fields:

> bibliographic titles (245, 246)
>
> uniform titles (130, 240, 440, 730)
>
> title portions of name/title headings (700, 800, 710, 810, 711, 811)

Therefore, you basically look for names in the name index and subjects in the subject index and titles in the title index, but you must be careful. There is no point looking in the name index for a heading that is in a 600 field, even if that heading is a name. A heading in a 600 field will be found in a subject index. In fact, a heading in any field beginning with 6 will be found in the subject index, even if that heading is a title.

Remember, if a heading is indexed (so that someone can search by it), then it must also be displayed (so the searcher does not have to wonder how he found what he did). Let's look at MARC coding for headings in more detail.

Tags for Personal Name Headings   X00

We begin with the MARC fields that contain personal names. Remember, the MARC tags for all personal names end in 00.

Let us try a *name* browse search on "lewis, c. s. clive staples" (see fig. 7-3).[1]

Fig. 7-3 ■ A Name Browse Search for C.S. Lewis at LC

Database Name: Library of Congress Online Catalog
YOU SEARCHED: Name Browse = lewis, c.s. clive staples
SEARCH RESULTS: Displaying 1 through 25 of 25.

◀ Previous   Next ▶

#	Titles	Headings	Heading Type
1	270	Lewis, C. S. (Clive Staples), 1898-1963	personal name

This search finds matching headings in MARC fields 100, 700, and 800:

```
100 1  $aLewis, C. S.$q(Clive Staples),$d1898-1963.
```

```
700 12 $aLewis, C. S.$q(Clive Staples),$d1898-1963.
```

```
800 1  $aLewis, C. S.$q(Clive Staples),$d1898-1963.$tChronicles of Narnia ;$v2.
```

We will now take a look at each of these personal name fields in more detail.

Personal Name—Main Entry   100

As we said earlier, our name browse search on "lewis, c. s. clive staples" matches headings in the 100 field:

```
100 1  $aLewis, C. S.$q(Clive Staples),$d1898-1963.
```

The 100 field (see table 7-1) contains the name of the person who is solely or primarily responsible for the intellectual and/or artistic content of the work being described. Remember, we call this a *main entry* field because of this concept of sole or primary responsibility.

Table 7-1 ■ 100 Coding

100	Personal main entry
Rule	AACR 21 for choice, 22 for form
Repeatable	No
Indicator 1	Type of personal name:
	0 Forename
	1 Surname
Indicator 2	Undefined—Blank
Subfields	
$a	Name (surname and forenames)
$q	Qualification of name (fuller form)
$b	Numeration (of a king, a queen, a pope, etc.)
$c	Titles, and other words associated with the name
$d	Dates of birth, death, or flourishing

The 100 field is not repeatable, which means that a MARC record can only contain one 100 field. In fact, a MARC record can contain only one *main entry,* so it cannot have more than one 1XX field; that is, it can have a 100 *or* 110 *or* 111 *or* 130, or no 1XX at all, but it cannot have a 100 *and* a 110, etc.

The values for indicator position 1 specify whether the name is a forename only (e.g., Avi), a surname only (e.g., Seuss), or, most commonly, a surname with a forename (e.g., Sully, Sue).

Indicator position 2 currently has no values—it is undefined in MARCspeak (it did have values at one time, but those values are now obsolete, so this position is now left blank).

Subfield $a contains the person's name (e.g., $aAvi; $aSeuss; $aSully, Sue; $aLewis, C. S.).

Subfields qbcd (notice that they are not in alphabetical order, but appear in the order in which they are to be entered) are for additions to a name to distinguish that name from the same name belonging to a different person, if it is necessary to do so. Study the following examples, looking up the meaning of each subfield in the chart shown in table 7-1:

```
100 0   $aAvi,$d1937-
```

```
100 1   $aSeuss,$cDr.
```

```
100 1   $aLewis, C. S.$q(Clive Staples),$d1898-1963.
```

```
100 0   $aElizabeth$bII,$cQueen of Great Britain,$d1926-
```

```
100 1   $aSully, Sue.
```

Notice the punctuation that precedes these additional subfields. This is the ISBD punctuation, prescribed by the cataloging rules that we mentioned in chapter 6.[2]

Personal Name Added Entry **700**

Our *name* browse search on "lewis, c. s. clive staples" will also find matching headings in the MARC 700 field:

```
245 00 $aPatterns of love and courtesy :$bessays in memory of C.S. Lewis.
700 1  $aLewis, C. S.$q(Clive Staples),$d1898-1963.
```

A 700 field (see table 7-2) contains the name of a person *also* responsible for, or related in some way to, the work being described; thus, it is called an "added" entry. The essays in the preceding example are not *by* C.S. Lewis, but he is related to the work because someone gathered those essays together in his memory. Because someone might think of searching for this book under his name, we make an added entry for him.

Table 7-2 ■ 700 Coding

700	Personal added entry
Rule	AACR 21 for choice, and 22 for form
Repeatable	Yes
Indicator 1	Type of personal name
0	Forename
1	Surname
Indicator 2	Type of added entry
#	Not analytic
2	Analytic
Subfields	
$a	Name (surname and forenames)
$q	Qualification of name (fuller form)
$b	Numeration (of a king, a queen, a pope, etc.)
$c	Titles, and other words associated with the name
$d	Dates of birth, death, or flourishing
$t	Title of work

Notice that:

Field 700 is repeatable, which means that a MARC record can contain as many 700 fields as the cataloger feels are needed.

Indicator 1 in the 700 means the same as in the 100 (type of name).

Indicator 2 in the 700 has a different meaning than in the 100; here it indicates whether the added entry applies to the whole work (e.g., contains the name of an editor of a work), or to just a part of the work (e.g., contains the author of a short story in a collection of short stories by multiple authors).

The subfield codes aqbc$d in the 700 mean the same as in the 100.

We have added subfield $t to our list. It contains the title of a work that was created by the person entered in subfield $a, and is used when we are referring to the work itself, not to the person who created the work. For example:

```
245 04  $aThe Lion, the witch and the wardrobe$h[videorecording] /$ca BBC-TV
          production in association with WonderWorks.
500     $aBased on the novel by C.S. Lewis.
700 1   $aLewis, C. S.$q(Clive Staples),$d1898-1963.$tLion, the witch and the
          wardrobe.
```

Personal Name Series Added Entry   800

Our name browse search on "lewis, c.s. clive staples" will also find matching records with this heading in MARC field 800:

```
800 1   $aLewis, C. S.$q(Clive Staples),$d1898-1963.$tChronicles of Narnia.
```

An 800 field (see table 7-3) contains the name of the person responsible for every work in a series, with the title of the series being entered in subfield $t.

Table 7-3 ■ 800 Coding

800	Personal series added entry
Rule	AACR 21 for choice and 22 for form
Repeatable	Yes
Indicator 1	Type of personal name
0	Forename
1	Surname
Indicator 2	Undefined—Blank
Subfields	
$a	Name (surname and forenames)
$q	Qualification of name (fuller form)
$b	Numeration (of a king, a queen, a pope, etc.)
$c	Titles, and other words associated with the name
$d	Dates of birth, death, or flourishing
$t	Title of work
$v	Volume or series number

Notice that:

Field 800 is repeatable, like the 700.

Indicator 1 in the 800 means the same as in the 100 and the 700 (type of name).

Indicator 2 in the 800 means the same as in the 100 (nothing), but has a different meaning than in the 700.

The subfield codes aqbc$d in the 800 mean the same as in the 100 and the 700.

We can include $t for a title as in the 700, but here it refers to the title of a series, not to the title of a related work.

We can add another subfield, $v, which contains the number of the particular volume of the item that we are describing, if it has a number.

```
800 1   $aLewis, C. S.$q(Clive Staples),$d1898-1963.$tChronicles of Narnia ;$v2.
```

Personal Name Subject Heading   600

Now, let us try a *subject* browse search on "lewis, c. s. clive staples" (see fig. 7-4). This finds our heading in the MARC 600 field:

```
600 10  $aLewis, C. S.$q(Clive Staples),$d1898-1963$xAppreciation.
```

Fig. 7-4 ■ A Subject Browse Search for C.S. Lewis at LC

Database Name: Library of Congress Online Catalog
YOU SEARCHED: Subject Browse = lewis, c.s. clive staples
SEARCH RESULTS: Displaying 1 through 25 of 25.

◀ Previous   Next ▶

#	Titles	Headings	Heading Type
1	49	Lewis, C. S. (Clive Staples), 1898-1963	LC subject headings

The 600 field (see table 7-4) contains the name of a person who is the subject of the work being described, e.g., a book of literary essays *about* C.S. Lewis.

Table 7-4 ■ 600 Coding

600	Personal subject heading
Rule	LCSH for choice; AACR 22 for form
Repeatable	Yes
Indicator 1	Type of personal name
0	Forename
1	Surname
3	Family name
Indicator 2	Source of subject heading
0	LCSH
1	Children's Annotated Headings
2	MeSH (National Library of Medicine)
3	National Library of Agriculture
4	Local heading
5	National Library of Canada (English)
6	National Library of Canada (French)
7	Source specified in $2
Subfields	
$a	Name (surname and forenames)
$q	Qualification of name (fuller form)
$b	Numeration (of a king, a queen, a pope, etc.)
$c	Titles, and other words associated with the name
$d	Dates of birth, death, or flourishing
$t	Title of work
$v	Form subdivision (what the work *is*)
$x	Topical subdivision (what the work is *about*)
$y	Chronological subdivision
$z	Geographic subdivision
$2	Source of subject heading or term

Notice that:

Field 600 is also repeatable, like the 700 and the 800.

Indicator 1 in the 600 means the same as in the 100, the 700, and the 800 (type of name), but here we have an additional value (3), which indicates that the heading is for a family name, not an individual (appropriate only for subject headings).

Indicator 2 in the 600 has a different meaning than in the 100, the 700, and the 800—it tells the source of the controlled vocabulary from which the subject heading was taken.

The subfield codes aqbc$d in the 600 mean the same as in the 100, the 700, and the 800.

Subfield $v here has a different meaning than in the 800; here, it is a **form subdivision.**

We added three additional subfields for **subject subdivisions** (xy$z).

We can use $t to refer to titles that are subjects.

We use a special subfield, $2, to say where the subject came from, if it did not come from one of the sources indicated by the second indicator.

Reviewing the MARC data elements in personal name headings (X00), we can see that:

Fields 600, 700, and 800 are repeatable; field 100 is not.

Indicator 1 has the same meaning in each field.

Indicator 2 has the same meaning in 100 and 800, and a different meaning in 600 and 700.

Subfields aqbc$d have the same meaning in each X00 field.

Other subfield values differ in meaning, depending on the type of heading involved.

This first detailed look at MARC coding in practice illustrates two general truths about MARC:

1. There is a certain pattern or symmetry to MARC coding.
2. We must be careful not to push the idea of that symmetry too far!

Tags for Corporate Name Headings   X10

In cataloging, the term *corporate bodies* refers to both businesses (IBM, Microsoft) and government agencies (U.S. Supreme Court, Florida Department of Fisheries). It can also refer to many other things that ordinarily we might not think of as corporate bodies: arboretums, bus terminals, castles, grain elevators, herbariums, lighthouses, nuclear power stations, planetariums, railroads, religious denominations, satellites, and theater companies, to name just a few. To help us to figure out what is to be coded as a corporate body (as defined by MARC), catalogers rely on something called the *List of Ambiguous Headings.*[3]

Try to remember that tags for corporate bodies all end in 10.

The coding for *corporate* name headings (X10) follows patterns that are very similar to the ones that we have just explained for *personal* name headings (X00). Because we are not trying to teach you coding at this point, it is those patterns that we want to emphasize. We suggest, therefore, that you concentrate in this section on the similarities between the coding for the two types of name headings (X00 and X10). For example, notice that:

110 (main entries) are not repeatable, just like 100.

610 (subject added entries), 710 (added entries), and 810 (series added entries) are repeatable, just like 600, 700 and 800.

In all X10, indicator 1 tells us what type of name is contained in the field, just like it does for X00.

In 110 and 810, indicator 2 is blank and undefined, like it is in 100 and 800.

In 610, indicator 2 tells us where the subject headings come from, just like it does for 600.

In 710, indicator 2 tells us whether the added entry applies to the whole work or just a part of the work, just like it does for 700.

The name subfields (ab) are the same in all X10 fields, just as the name subfields (aqbc$d) are the same in all X00 fields.

We can add the same title subfield ($t) to X10 as we can to X00.

We can add the same series number subfield ($v) to X10 as we can to X00.

We can add the same subject subfields (xvyz) to X10 as we can to X00.

If you are interested, you may read on to find out more about the coding of corporate name headings but, at this point, the most important thing for you to realize is that these very useful patterns are present in the coding for both personal and corporate name headings.

A name browse search on "national library of australia" (see fig. 7-5) will find matching headings in MARC fields 110, 710, and 810:

```
110 2   $aNational Library of Australia.
```

```
710 2   $aNational Library of Australia.
```

```
810 2   $aNational Library of Australia.$tNLA today ;$vno. 1.
```

Fig. 7-5 ■ A Name Browse Search for "National Library of Australia" at LC

Database Name: Library of Congress Online Catalog
YOU SEARCHED: Name Browse = national library of australia
SEARCH RESULTS: Displaying 1 through 25 of 25.

◀ Previous   Next ▶

#	Titles	Headings	Heading Type
[MORE INFO] 1	184	National Library of Australia.	corporate name

We will now take a look at each of these corporate name fields in more detail.

Corporate Name Main Entry   110

As a main entry, the 110 field (see table 7-5) contains the name of the corporate body primarily responsible for the intellectual and/or artistic content of the work being described. Like the other main entry fields (100, 111, 130), the 110 field is not repeatable.

Table 7-5 ■ 110 Coding

110	Corporate main entry
Rule	AACR 21 for choice and 23 or 24 for form
Repeatable	No
Indicator 1	Type of corporate name
1	Place or place and name
2	Name (direct order)
Indicator 2	Undefined—Blank
Subfields	
$a	Name of corporate body
$b	Each subordinate unit in the hierarchy of the corporate body

Indicator 1 specifies whether the name of the institution begins with a place name, i.e., is for a government entity (e.g., Florida. Division of Tourism), or doesn't begin with a place name (e.g., Envirocycle Systems).

Subfield $a contains the name of the top-level institution or government (e.g., $aFlorida or $aEnvirocycle Systems).

Subfield $b contains the name of a **subordinate body,** often a department or division of the parent body:

```
110 1   $aFlorida.$bDivision of Tourism.
```

```
110 2   $aEnvirocycle Systems.
```

Government names sometimes require several subfield $b's in order to delineate the hierarchy and zero in on the specific agency being referred to:

```
110 1   $aUnited States.$bDept. of Agriculture.$bEconomic Research
        Service.$bAfrica and Middle East Branch.
```

Corporate Name Added Entry   710

Our name browse search on "national library of australia" will also find matching headings in the MARC 710 field:

```
710 2   $aNational Library of Australia.
```

The 710 field (see table 7-6) contains the name of a corporate body that is also related in some way to the work being described; thus, it is called an *added entry.* The 710 field is repeatable, so a cataloger can enter as many as he or she feels are necessary for patron access.

Table 7-6 ■ **710 Coding**

710	Corporate added entry
Rule	AACR 21 for choice and 23 or 24 for form
Repeatable	Yes
Indicator 1	Type of corporate name
1	Place or place and name
2	Name (direct order)
Indicator 2	Type of added entry
#	Not analytic
2	Analytic
Subfields	
$a	Name of corporate body
$b	Each subordinate unit in the hierarchy of the corporate body
$t	Title of work

Notice that:

>   Indicator 1 in the 710 means the same as in the 110.

>   Indicator 2 in the 710 has a different meaning than in the 110, but means the same as in the 700—it indicates whether the added entry applies to the whole work or to just a part of the work. (Indicator 2 has the same meaning for all 7XX fields.)

>   The subfield codes ab in the 710 mean the same as in the 110.

>   As we did for the 700, we also add subfield $t to our list for the 710; $t contains the title of the work of a **name/title added entry,** e.g.:

```
710 1   $aUnited States.$bDept. of State.$tDepartment of State Bulletin.
```

Corporate Name Series Added Entry   *810*

Our name browse search on "national library of australia" will also find matching headings in MARC field 810:

```
810 2   $aNational Library of Australia.$tNLA today ;$vno. 1.
```

An 810 field (see table 7-7) contains the name of the corporate body responsible for every work in a series, with the title of the series being given in the $t.

Notice that:

>   Indicator 1 in the 810 means the same as in the 110 and the 710.

>   Indicator 2 in the 810 means the same as in the 110 (nothing), but has a different meaning than in the 710.

>   The subfield codes ab in the 810 mean the same as in the 110 and the 710.

>   We can add $t for a title again, this time for the title of the series.

Table 7-7 ▪ 810 Coding

810	Corporate name series added entry
Rule	AACR 21 for choice and 23 or 24 for form
Repeatable	Yes
Indicator 1	Type of corporate name
1	Place or place and name
2	Name (direct order)
Indicator 2	Undefined
Subfields	
$a	Name of corporate body
$b	Each subordinate unit in the hierarchy of the corporate body
$t	Title of work
$v	Volume or series number

We can add subfield $v, which contains the number of the particular volume of the item that we are describing, if it has a number. (All series fields use subfield $v for this purpose.)

Corporate Name Subject Heading   610

Let's try a subject browse search on "national library of australia" (see fig. 7-6).

Fig. 7-6 ▪ A Subject Browse Search for "National Library of Australia" at LC

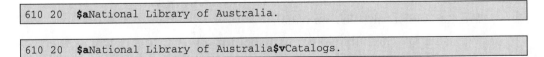

Database Name: Library of Congress Online Catalog
YOU SEARCHED: Subject Browse = national library of australia
SEARCH RESULTS: Displaying 1 through 25 of 25.

◄ Previous   Next ►

#	Titles	Headings	Heading Type
[MORE INFO] 1	26	National Library of Australia.	LC subject headings

This will find this heading in MARC field 610:

```
610 20   $aNational Library of Australia.
```

```
610 20   $aNational Library of Australia$vCatalogs.
```

A 610 field (see table 7-8) contains the name of a corporate body that is the subject of the work being described, e.g., a video about the National Library of Australia.

Table 7-8 ■ 610 Coding

610	Corporate subject heading
Rule	LCSH for choice; AACR 23 or 24 for form
Repeatable	Yes
Indicator 1	Type of corporate name
1	Place or place and name
2	Name (direct order)
Indicator 2	Source of subject heading
0	LCSH
1	Children's Annotated Headings
2	MeSH (National Library of Medicine)
3	National Library of Agriculture
4	Local heading
5	National Library of Canada (English)
6	National Library of Canada (French)
7	Source specified in $2
Subfields	
$a	Name of corporate body
$b	Each subordinate unit in the hierarchy of the corporate body
$t	Title of work
$v	Form subdivision
$x	Topical subdivision
$y	Chronological subdivision
$z	Geographic subdivision
$2	Source of subject heading or term

Notice that:

Indicator 1 in the 610 has the same meaning as it did in the other X10 fields (110, 710, and 810).

Indicator 2 in the 610 has a different meaning than in the 110, the 710, and the 810, but means the same as in the 600: it tells us where the subject heading comes from. (Indicator 2 has the same meaning in all 6XX fields.)

The subfield codes ab in the 610 mean the same as in the 110, the 710, and the 810.

The subfield $v in a 610 is for a subject subdivision, and we have three additional subfields for subject subdivisions (xy$z). (These four subdivision subfields are valid for all 6XX fields.)

We can use $t for titles, as usual.

We use a special subfield $2, as usual for all 6XX, to say where the subject heading came from, if not from one of the sources specified by I2.

So, to review the corporate name fields (X10):

Fields 610, 710, and 810 are repeatable; field 110 is not.

Indicator 1 has the same meaning in all X10 fields.

Indicator 2 has the same meaning in the 110 and the 810 and a different meaning in the 610 and the 710.

Subfields ab have the same meaning in each X10 field.

Other subfield values differ in meaning depending on the type of heading involved.

Tags for Conference Name Headings   X11

The term *conference* when applied to a heading includes conferences, meetings, conventions, exhibitions, expeditions, folk festivals, fairs, parades, public celebrations, races, and sporting events. The *List of Ambiguous Headings* mentioned in the preceding section on corporate names is also used by catalogers to decide on coding for a heading for a conference. Try to remember that tags for all conferences end in 11.

Like the coding for *corporate* name headings (X10) the coding for *conference* name headings (X11) also follows patterns very similar to the coding for *personal* name headings (X00). Again, it is those patterns that we want to emphasize. We suggest, therefore, that you concentrate in this section on the similarities between the coding for the three types of name headings (X00, X10, and X11). For example, notice that:

111 (main entries) are not repeatable, just like 100 and 110.

611 (subject added entries), 711 (added entries), and 811 (series added entries) are repeatable, just like 600, 700, and 800 and 610, 710, and 810.

In all X11, indicator 1 tells us what type of name is contained in the field, just like it does for X00 and X10.

In 111 and 811, indicator 2 is blank and undefined, just like it is in 100, 110, 800, and 810.

In 611, indicator 2 tells us where the subject headings come from, just like it does for 600 and 610.

In 711, indicator 2 tells us whether the added entry applies to the whole work or just a part of the work, just like it does for 700 and 710.

The name subfields (andc) are the same in all X11 fields, just as the name subfields (aqbc$d) are the same in all X00 fields and the name subfields (ab) are the same in all X10 fields.

We can add the same title subfield ($t) to X11 as we can to X00 and X10.

We can add the same series number subfield ($v) to X11 as we can to X00 and X10.

We can add the same subject subfields (xvyz) to X11 as we can to X00 and X10.

If you are interested, you may now read more about the coding of conference name headings, but once again remember that for now the most important thing to grasp is that there are these marvelous patterns woven through the coding of all name headings.

Conference Name Main Entry   111

A name browse search on "pannonian symposium on mathematical statistics" (see fig. 7-7) will find matching headings in MARC fields 111, 711, and 811:

Fig. 7-7 ■ A Name Browse Search for "Pannonian Symposium on Mathematical Statistics" at LC

Database Name: Library of Congress Online Catalog
YOU SEARCHED: Name Browse = pannonian symposium on mathematical statistics 4th
SEARCH RESULTS: Displaying 1 through 25 of 25.

◄ Previous   Next ►

#	Titles	Headings	Heading Type
1	1	Pannonian Symposium on Mathematical Statistics (1981 : Bad Tatzmannsdorf, Austria)	meeting name

```
111 2   $aPannonian Symposium on Mathematical Statistics$n(4th :$d1983 :$cBad
        Tatzmannsdorf, Austria)
```

```
711 2   $aPannonian Symposium on Mathematical Statistics$n(4th :$d1983 :$cBad
        Tatzmannsdorf, Austria)
```

```
811 2   $aPannonian Symposium on Mathematical Statistics$n(4th :$d1983 :$cBad
        Tatzmannsdorf, Austria).$tProceedings of the 4th Pannonian Symposium
        on Mathematical Statistics, Bad Tatzmannsdorf, Austria, 4-10 September
        1983 ;$vv. B.
```

Notice that the 111 field (see table 7-9) contains the name of the conference, meeting, event, etc., reported on by the work being described. Like all 1XX fields, the 111 is not repeatable.

Table 7-9 ■ 111 Coding

111	Conference main entry
Rule	AACR 21 for choice and 24 for form
Repeatable	No
Indicator 1	Type of conference name
2	Name (direct order)
Indicator 2	Undefined—Blank
Subfields	
$a	Name of meeting
$n	Number of meeting
$d	Date of meeting
$c	Place of meeting

Indicator 1 has only one value and indicates that the name of the conference is given in direct order.[4] Indicator 2 is undefined.

Subfield $a contains the name of the conference, meeting, event, etc. (e.g., $aOlympic Games).

Subfields $n (the number of a meeting), $d (the year in which the meeting was held), and $c (the place in which the meeting was held) are used to distinguish a meeting or conference from another meeting or conference with the same name, if it is necessary to do so, e.g.:

```
111  2   $aOlympic Games$n(10th  :$d1932  :$cLos Angeles, Calif.)
```

```
111  2   $aOlympic Games$n(11th  :$d1936  :$cBerlin, Germany)
```

Conference Name Added Entry   711

Our name browse search on "pannonian symposium . . ." will also find matching headings in MARC field 711:

```
711  2   $aPannonian Symposium on Mathematical Statistics$n(4th  :$d1983  :$cBad
             Tatzmannsdorf, Austria)
```

The 711 field (see table 7-10) contains the name of a conference, a meeting, an event, etc., connected in some way to the work being described.

Table 7-10 ▪ 711 Coding

711	Conference added entry
Rule	AACR 21 for choice and 24 for form
Repeatable	Yes
Indicator 1	Type of conference name
2	Name (direct order)
Indicator 2	Type of added entry
#	Not analytic
2	Analytic
Subfields	
$a	Name of meeting
$n	Number of meeting
$d	Date of meeting
$c	Place of meeting
$t	Title of work

Notice that:

Indicator 1 in the 711 has the same meaning as in the 111 field (type of name).

Indicator 2 in the 711 has a different meaning than in the 111, but means the same as it does in all 7XX headings fields—it indicates whether the added entry applies to the whole work or to just a part of the work.

The subfield codes andc have the same meanings as in the 111 field.

As in the 700 and the 710 fields, we have a subfield $t in the 711, and it again contains the title of the work in a name/title added entry.

Conference Name Series Added Entry   811

Our example name browse search on "pannonian symposium . . ." will also find matching headings in MARC field 811:

```
811 2   $aPannonian Symposium on Mathematical Statistics$n(4th  :$d1983  :$cBad
        Tatzmannsdorf, Austria).$tProceedings of the 4th Pannonian Symposium
        on Mathematical Statistics, Bad Tatzmannsdorf, Austria, 4-10 September
        1983 ;$vv. B.
```

The 811 field (see table 7-11) contains the name of the conference, meeting, event, etc., responsible for every work in a series, with the title of the series in subfield $t.

Table 7-11 ■ 811 Coding

811	Conference series added entry
Rule	AACR 21 for choice and 24 for form
Repeatable	Yes
Indicator 1	Type of conference name
2	Name (direct order)
Indicator 2	Undefined—Blank
Subfields	
$a	Name of meeting
$n	Number of meeting
$d	Date of meeting
$c	Place of meeting
$t	Title of series
$v	Volume or series number

Notice that:

Indicator 1 in the 811 means the same as in the 111 and the 711 (type of name).

Indicator 2 in the 811 means the same as in the 111 (undefined), but has a different meaning than in the 711.

The subfield codes andc have the same meanings as in the 111 and the 711.

We can add subfields $t and $v, just as we did for series in the 800 and the 810:

- $t contains the title of the series.

- $v contains the number of the particular volume of the item that we are describing, if it has a number.

Conference Name Subject Heading   611

Finally, a subject browse search on a different conference heading, "centennial exhibition 1876" (see fig. 7-8), will find matching headings in MARC field 611:

Fig. 7-8 ■ A Subject Browse Search for "Centennial Exhibition 1876" at LC

Database Name: Library of Congress Online Catalog
YOU SEARCHED: Subject Browse = centennial exhibition 1876
SEARCH RESULTS: Displaying 1 through 25 of 25.

◀ Previous   Next ▶

#	Titles	Headings	Heading Type
1	75	Centennial Exhibition (1876 : Philadelphia, Pa.)	LC subject headings
2	5	Centennial Exhibition (1876 : Philadelphia, Pa.) Aerial views.	LC subject headings

```
611 20 $aCentennial Exhibition$d(1876 :$cPhiladelphia, Pa.)
```

```
611 20 $aCentennial Exhibition$d(1876 :$cPhiladelphia, Pa.)$vAerial views.
```

The 611 field (see table 7-12) contains the name of a conference, a meeting, an event, etc., that is the subject of the work being described, e.g., an electronic resource about the Olympic Games.

Table 7-12 ■ 611 Coding

611	Conference subject heading
Rule	LCSH for choice; AACR 24 for form
Repeatable	Yes
Indicator 1	Type of conference name
2	Name (direct order)
Indicator 2	Source of subject heading
0	LCSH
1	Children's Annotated Headings
2	MeSH (National Library of Medicine)
3	National Library of Agriculture
4	Local heading
5	National Library of Canada (English)
6	National Library of Canada (French)
7	Source specified in $2
Subfields	
$a	Name of meeting
$n	Number of meeting
$d	Date of meeting
$c	Place of meeting
$t	Title of series
$v	Form subdivision
$x	Topical subdivision
$y	Chronological subdivision
$z	Geographic subdivision
$2	Source of subject heading or term

Notice that:

> Indicator 1 in the 611 has the same meaning as in the other X11 fields (111, 711, and 811—type of name).

> Indicator 2 in the 611 has a different meaning than in the other X11 fields, but means the same as in the other 6XX fields—it tells us where the subject heading comes from.

> The subfield codes andc have the same meaning as in the 111, the 711, and the 811.

> The $v here has the same meaning as it has in all subject fields (6XX)—form subdivision.

> We also have the three additional subfields for subject subdivisions (xy$z).

> We can use $t for titles, as usual.

> We again use a special subfield $2, as we can for all 6XX fields, to say where the subject heading came from, if the source is not one of those specified by I2.

So, for all these conference name headings (X11), we can say that:

> Fields 611, 711, and 811 are repeatable; 111 is not.

> Indicator 1 has the same meaning in all X11 fields.

> Indicator 2 has the same meaning in the 111 and the 811 and a different meaning in the 611 and the 711.

> Subfields andc have the same meanings in each X11 field.

Other subfield values have different meanings depending on the type of heading involved.

Tags for Uniform Title Headings   X30

A uniform title is needed sometimes in order to:

> bring together all catalog entries for a work that has appeared under various titles (e.g., because of different editions or translations); or

> add something to the title of a work to distinguish it from a different work with the same title.

First, we present a real-world example to show you just how useful the uniform title can be. Consider the play we know as *Hamlet*. Various editions of Shakespeare's drama can be found in the OPAC at LC under such titles as:

> [The] first edition of the tragedy of Hamlet

> Hamlet, Prince of Denmark

> Historie of Hamlet, Prince of Denmarke

> Shakespeare's Hamlet

> Tragedia de Hamlet, principe da Dinamarca

> [The] tragedie of Hamlet, Prince of Denmark

> [The] tragedy of Hamlet, Prince of Denmark

[The] tragicall historie of Hamlet, Prince of Denmarke

Tragique histoire de Hamlet prince de Danemark

Tragische Geschichte von Hamlet, Prinzen von Daenemark

In some cases, there is just a slight variation in spelling between the titles; in others, there is a significant difference in where the heading for the title would file in a catalog. The uniform title "Hamlet" will collect all the preceding variations—and the many others that we have not listed—under a single heading in the catalog. The patron who enters "Hamlet" will, thus, find all the relevant works. Such is the good work performed for us by a uniform title.

Try to remember that the MARC tags for all uniform titles end in 30, except the 240 tag, but we will say more on the 240 in a bit.

Uniform Title Main Entry   130

A title browse search for "bible n.t. mark" (see fig. 7-9) will find it in MARC field 130:

```
130 0   $aBible.$pN.T.$pMark.
```

Fig. 7-9 ■ A Title Browse Search for "Bible N.T. Mark" at LC

Database Name: Library of Congress Online Catalog
YOU SEARCHED: Title = bible n.t. mark
SEARCH RESULTS: Displaying 1 through 25 of 333.

◄ Previous   Next ►

#	Title	Name: Main Author, Creator, etc.	Full Title	Date
☐ 1	Bible. N.T. Mark.		Book of Mark [sound recording] : paraphrased Scripture in song.	1992
☐ 2	Bible. N.T. Mark.	Bratcher, Robert G.	Translator's guide to the Gospel of Mark / by Robert G. Bratcher.	1981
☐ 3	Bible. N.T. Mark.	Dumitriu, Petru.	Comment ne pas l'aimer! : une lecture de l'Evangile selon saint Marc / par Petru Dumitriu.	1981

The 130 field (see table 7-13) contains the established title of the work, when it does not have a personal name, corporate name, or conference name as the main entry. On the other hand, if you do have a main entry (like a 100) and still need to add a uniform title, you must use MARC tag 240 instead (see the following section).

Indicator 1 is a **filing indicator** and specifies the number of characters that the system must skip before it begins indexing the title (see the I2 under 245 in

Table 7-13 ■ 130 Coding

130	Uniform title main entry
Rule	AACR 21 for choice and 25 for form
Repeatable	No
Indicator 1	Filing indicator
0–9	Nonfiling characters to skip before beginning indexing
Indicator 2	Undefined—Blank
Subfields	
$a	Uniform title
$n	Numbered part or section
$p	Named part or section
$l	Language of work
$s	Version
$f	Date of work

the display section of chapter 8 for more details). However, the 1993 amendments to the cataloging rules (AACR) say that we are to omit **initial articles** *in uniform titles* (unless we want to file under those initial articles), so the value of this indicator position for uniform titles is now always 0. Indicator 2 is undefined, as for all 1XX fields.

Notice that:

> The subfield coding for uniform titles introduces some codes that are different from what we have seen so far in headings. Subfield $a, of course, contains the uniform title of the work (e.g., Hamlet, Bible).

> The other subfields contain additions to the uniform title to distinguish it from the same title belonging to a different work, if it is necessary to do so, e.g.:

```
130 0   $aBible.$pO.T.$pJob.$lEnglish.$sNew English.
```

```
130 0   $aBible.$pO.T.$pKings, 1st XIX, 4-18.$lGerman.$sLuther.$f1921.
```

By the way, if you ever dig more deeply into MARC coding, you will see that all these additional uniform title subfields can be tacked onto titles in name/title added entries.

Uniform Title   240

Tag 130 is used for the uniform title of a work that does not have a personal, corporate, or conference "author" main entry. However, we need a way in MARC to code a uniform title for a work that does have such an "author," and, thus, we come to tag 240. Let's try a title browse search for "Hamlet" (see fig. 7-10). This search finds matching headings in MARC field 240:

```
100 1   $aShakespeare, William,$d1564-1616.
240 10 $aHamlet
```

Fig. 7-10 ■ A Title Browse Search for "Hamlet" at LC

Database Name: Library of Congress Online Catalog
YOU SEARCHED: Title = hamlet
SEARCH RESULTS: Displaying 226 through 250 of 845.

◀ Previous   Next ▶

#	Title	Name: Main Author, Creator, etc.	Full Title	Date
☐ 226	Hamlet	Shakespeare, William, 1564-1616.	Tragedy of Hamlet [computer file] / by William Shakespeare.	1994
☐ 227	Hamlet	Shakespeare, William, 1564-1616.	Tragedy of Hamlet / edited by Edward Dowden.	1899
☐ 228	Hamlet	Shakespeare, William, 1564-1616.	Tragedy of Hamlet, Prince of Denmark.	1966

Hamlet, of course, has an author, Shakespeare, whose name will appear as the main entry in the 100 field of the record. Because a 100 field is already present in the record and we cannot have two 1XX fields in a record, we use the 240 field for the uniform title.

By the way, the 240 field, like a 1XX tag, is nonrepeatable (see table 7-14), and it is also not valid to enter a 130 (uniform title main entry) and a 240 (uniform title) in the same record.

Table 7-14 ■ 240 Coding

240	Uniform title main entry
Rule	AACR 21 for choice and 25 for form
Repeatable	No
Indicator 1	Display indicator
0	Do not print/Display the field
1	Print/Display the field
Indicator 2	Filing indicator
0–9	Nonfiling characters to skip before beginning indexing
Subfields	
$a	Title
$n	Numbered part or section
$p	Named part or section
$l	Language of work
$s	Version
$f	Date of work

Notice that:

The coding for MARC field 240 is exactly the same as the coding for MARC field 130, except for the indicators. Indicator 1 in the 240 field tells the system whether to display the field (the default) or to suppress display, and indicator 2 tells the system how many characters to skip before indexing the title.

Here is another example of using a 240 instead of a 130. The *Iliad* is by Homer, so if we want to gather all versions of the *Iliad* together, we have to use a 240 for the uniform title, because "Homer" will be in the 100 field as the author for this work (and we can have only one 1XX field in a record). Now suppose we want to indicate specifically which version of the *Iliad* we have. We give the uniform title in $a and then add whatever we need to specify exactly which part and version of the work we have in our collection. The following example illustrates the use of subfield $n, to show that this work includes only Books 1–6, not the complete *Iliad,* and the $f shows the date of publication of this particular version:

```
240 10 $aIliad.$nBook 1-6.$f1889.
```

Uniform Title Added Entry   730

The title browse search on "bible n.t. mark" that we demonstrated earlier for field 130 will also find matching headings in MARC field 730:

```
730 02 $aBible.$pN.T.$pMatthew.
730 02 $aBible.$pN.T.$pMark.
730 02 $aBible.$pN.T.$pLuke.
730 02 $aBible.$pN.T.$pJohn.
```

The 730 field (see table 7-15) contains the title of a work that is related in some way to the work being described. For example, the 730 field could be used for the title of a work on which a movie being described in the record is based, if the work did not have a personal, corporate, or conference "author"; or, as the I2 indicates for this example, a 730 could be used for the title of a work that is included in a collection of works.

Table 7-15 ■ 730 Coding

730	Uniform title added entry
Rule	AACR 21 for choice and 25 for form
Repeatable	Yes
Indicator 1	Filing indicator
0–9	Nonfiling characters to skip before beginning indexing
Indicator 2	Type of added entry
#	Not analytic
2	Analytic
Subfields	
$a	Title
$n	Numbered part or section
$p	Named part or section
$l	Language of work
$s	Version
$f	Date of work

Notice that:

>The only difference in the MARC coding between the 130 and the 730 fields is the use of indicator 2 in the 730, which has the same meaning as it does in all 7XX tags: it indicates whether the added entry applies to the whole work, e.g., a related work, or just to a part of the work, e.g., a story in a collection.

Uniform Title Series Added Entry *830*

A different title browse search on "problems in american civilization" (see fig. 7-11) will find matching headings in MARC field 830:

```
830  0    $aProblems in American civilization ;$v22.
```

Fig. 7-11 ■ A Title Browse Search for "Problems in American Civilization" at LC

Database Name: Library of Congress Online Catalog
YOU SEARCHED: Title = problems in american civilization
SEARCH RESULTS: Displaying 1 through 25 of 87.

◄ Previous   Next ►

#	Title	Name: Main Author, Creator, etc.	Full Title	Date
☐ 1	Problems in American civilization		Abolitionists : means, ends, and motivations / edited and with an introduction by Lawrence B. Goodheart, Hugh Hawkins.	1995
☐ 2	Problems in American civilization		American populism / edited and with an introduction by William F. Holmes.	1994

The 830 field (see table 7-16) contains the established title of a series that does not have a personal, corporate, or conference "author"; if it did have such an author, the series would be coded in an 800, 810, or 811 field, as previously outlined.

Table 7-16 ■ 830 Coding

830	Uniform title series added entry
Rule	AACR 21 for choice and 25 for form
Repeatable	Yes
Indicator 1	Undefined—Blank
Indicator 2	Filing Indicator
0–9	Nonfiling characters to skip before beginning indexing
Subfields	
$a	Title
$n	Numbered part or section
$p	Named part or section
$l	Language of work
$s	Version
$f	Date of work
$v	Volume or series number

Notice that:

> Indicator 1 in the 830 has the same meaning as indicator 2 in the 130 (undefined).
>
> Indicator 2 in the 830 has the same meaning as indicator 2 in the 240 (nonfiling characters).
>
> The subfield codes used in the 830 have the same meanings as they do in the other uniform title fields.

Uniform Title Subject Heading   630

A uniform title that has an author will be entered under the name of the author when that title is given as a subject heading and will be coded accordingly in the 6XX (600, 610, or 611), e.g.:

```
600 10 $aShakespeare, William,$d1564-1616.$tHamlet.
```

However, if a work without an author is the subject of another work, then it (the work that is the subject) is entered under its title and coded 630. The classic example of the use of a 630 tag would be for any work about the Bible or any other sacred scripture:

```
630 00 $aBible.$pN.T.$pMark$xBuddhist interpretations.
```

So, the 630 field (see table 7-17) contains the title of a work that is the subject of the work being described, when the described work has no personal, corporate, or conference author.

Notice that:

> Indicator 1 in the 630 means the same as I1 in the 130 and the 730 and I2 in the 240 and the 830 (nonfiling characters).

Table 7-17 ■ 630 Coding

630	Uniform title subject heading
Rule	LCSH for choice; AACR 25 for form
Repeatable	Yes
Indicator 1	Filing indicator
0–9	Nonfiling characters to skip before beginning indexing
Indicator 2	Source of subject heading
0	LCSH
1	Children's Annotated Headings
2	MeSH (National Library of Medicine)
3	National Library of Agriculture
4	Local heading
5	National Library of Canada (English)
6	National Library of Canada (French)
7	Source specified in $2
Subfields	
$a	Title
$n	Numbered part or section
$p	Named part or section
$l	Language of work
$s	Version
$f	Date of work
$v	Form subdivision
$x	Topical subdivision
$y	Chronological subdivision
$z	Geographic subdivision
$2	Source of subject heading or term

Indicator 2 in the 630 has a different meaning than in the 130, the 240, the 730, and the 830, but means the same as in the other 6XX fields—it tells us where the subject heading comes from; this is very important to remember.

The 630 also has the usual four subfields for subject subdivisions (vxyz).

We use the subfield $2, as usual, to say where the subject heading came from, if it did not come from one of the sources specified by the second indicator.

The remaining subfield codes in the 630 have the same meanings as they do in the other uniform title fields (130, 240, 730, and 830).

So, for all these uniform title headings (X30 and 240):

An indicator for nonfiling characters will be found in either I1 or I2. The meaning of the other indicator will vary from field to field. The indicators for uniform titles are pretty mixed up in this regard.

Subfields anplsf have the same meanings in each field.

Other subfields will differ, depending on the type of heading involved.

Tags for Other Subject Headings   6XX

Only a few fields are left before we can wrap up our discussion of indexed fields or headings. We have already seen that subject headings are always coded 6XX (600, 610, 611, and 630). Now let's have a look at the kinds of things that we usually think of as subject headings.

Topical Subject Heading   650

A subject browse search for "coral reef" (see fig. 7-12) will find matching headings in MARC field 650:

```
650 0  $aCoral reef animals.
650 1  $aCoral reef animals.
```

Fig. 7-12 ■ A Subject Browse Search for "Coral Reef" at LC

Database Name: Library of Congress Online Catalog
YOU SEARCHED: Subject Browse = coral reef
SEARCH RESULTS: Displaying 1 through 25 of 25.

◀ Previous   Next ▶

#	Titles	Headings	Heading Type
1	26	Coral reef animals	LC subject headings
2	15	Coral reef animals.	LC subject headings for children

This field (see table 7-18) contains a topical term that describes what the material being described is *about*.

Notice that:

> We use the same indicator 2 values for all subject headings (6XX—except 655), and the same subject subdivision subfields (vxyz) and source subfield $2.

Indicator 1 in the 650 field specifies whether the subject is a primary or secondary descriptor of the content of the described material. Unless you are cataloging technical reports, you will not need to code anything in this indicator and will almost always see it coded blank—no information provided—in any records that you copy.

Indicator 2, however, is very important, as it is for all 6XX fields. It indicates the source of the subject heading (as we have mentioned more than once already). Why is this important? Most systems are set up by default to index only LCSH headings (I2 = 0). If you add or create MARC records that have subject headings that are not LCSH, those non-LCSH headings may neither display in your catalog nor be indexed, because the system may only be looking for 6XX I2 = 0. Therefore, if you create local subject headings (I2 = 4) or use headings from

Table 7-18 ■ 650 Coding

650	Topical subject heading
Rule	LCSH for choice and form
Repeatable	Yes
Indicator 1	Level of subject term
#	No information provided
Indicator 2	Source of subject heading
0	LCSH
1	Children's Annotated Headings
2	MeSH (National Library of Medicine)
3	National Library of Agriculture
4	Local heading
5	National Library of Canada (English)
6	National Library of Canada (French)
7	Source specified in $2
Subfields	
$a	Topical heading
$v	Form subdivision
$x	Topical subdivision
$y	Chronological subdivision
$z	Geographic subdivision
$2	Source of subject heading or term

any "other" source (e.g., I2 = 1), you must be sure that your system is set up to recognize subject fields with the corresponding indicator 2 values. Otherwise there will be no subject access to those records for your patrons.

Geographic Subject Heading   651

A subject browse search on a place, such as "jamaica history 1962" (see fig. 7-13), will find matching headings in MARC field 651:

```
651 0   $aJamaica$xHistory$y1962-
651 0   $aJamaica$xHistory$y1962-$vCaricatures and cartoons.
```

Fig. 7-13 ■ A Subject Browse Search for "Jamaica History 1962" at LC

Database Name: Library of Congress Online Catalog
YOU SEARCHED: Subject Browse = jamaica history 1962
SEARCH RESULTS: Displaying 1 through 25 of 25.

◀ Previous   Next ▶

#	Titles	Headings	Heading Type
1	3	Jamaica History 1962-	LC subject headings
2	1	Jamaica History 1962- Caricatures and cartoons.	LC subject headings

The 651 field (see table 7-19) contains a geographic name that is used as a subject heading for the material being described. This field is coded exactly the same as the 650 (except that indicator 1 is *always* blank).

Table 7-19 ■ 651 Coding

651	Geographic subject heading
Rule	LCSH for choice and form
Repeatable	Yes
Indicator 1	Undefined—Blank
Indicator 2	Source of subject heading
0	LCSH
1	Children's Annotated Headings
2	MeSH (National Library of Medicine)
3	National Library of Agriculture
4	Local heading
5	National Library of Canada (English)
6	National Library of Canada (French)
7	Source specified in $2
Subfields	
$a	Geographic heading
$v	Form subdivision
$x	Topical subdivision
$y	Chronological subdivision
$z	Geographic subdivision
$2	Source of subject heading or term

Notice that:

We use the same indicator 2 values and the same subject subdivision subfields (vxyz) and $2 (source) for all subject headings (6XX).

Genre/Form Term   655

We will conclude our look at subject headings with a discussion of a tag that is somewhat new to MARC21, the 655 tag for a **genre/form heading.** A subject browse search for "allegories" (see fig. 7-14) will find matching headings in both MARC fields 650 and 655:

```
655 7   $aAllegories.$2gsafd
```

```
650 0   $aAllegories.
```

```
650 1   $aAllegories.
```

Fig. 7-14 ■ A Subject Browse Search for "Allegories" at LC

Database Name: Library of Congress Online Catalog
YOU SEARCHED: Subject Browse = allegories
SEARCH RESULTS: Displaying 1 through 25 of 25.

◄ Previous   Next ►

#	Titles	Headings	Heading Type
1	341	Allegories.	Guidelines on subj. access to works of fiction
[MORE INFO] 2	157	Allegories	LC subject headings
3	27	Allegories.	LC subject headings for children

The 655 field (see table 7-20) contains a term indicating the genre, form, and/or physical characteristics of the material being described.

Table 7-20 ■ 655 Coding

655	Genre/Form term
Rule	LCSH for choice and form
Repeatable	Yes
Indicator 1	Type of heading
#	Basic
0	Faceted (rare)
Indicator 2	Source of subject heading
7	Source specified in $2
Subfields	
$a	Genre/Form term
$v	Form subdivision
$x	Topical subdivision
$y	Chronological subdivision
$z	Geographic subdivision
$2	Source of term

Indicator 1 is usually blank. Indicator 2 is always 7, which means that the source of the heading is given in subfield $2, in a coded form. The other subfields are the same in the 655 as in other subject headings.

Why does our search find the same heading in three different MARC fields? First, the term *allegories* is both a valid LC subject heading (650 I2 = 0) and a valid LC children's heading (650 I2 = 1)—note the difference in the second indicators in these two examples. In these two instances, catalogers know that the second indicators are supposed to indicate that the work is *about* allegories. However, the term *allegories* is also a valid genre/form heading (655) when the work actually *is* an allegory.

The LC catalog indicates, in the column labeled "Heading Type," the fact that the same term comes from three different lists. However, this column does not really explain the differences in the meaning of the term (the first heading is for works that *are* allegories, the second heading is for *nonjuvenile* works *about* allegories, and the third heading is for *juvenile* works *about* allegories).

Most systems, however, do not even have this heading type column, but simply repeat the same heading in the browse list, much to the confusion of patrons. For example:

> Allegories. (371)
> Allegories. (156)
> Allegories. (27)

It is to be hoped that at some point our library automation system vendors will devise a way to let patrons know the difference between apparently duplicate headings. We know why we code them differently, but it would be good to let the patrons in on our secret.

As we said, 655 is a relatively new field, and you should find out if it is indexing and displaying in your system at all.

QUIZ 7

1. What tag would I use for a:

   Personal name main entry? _____

   Corporate name added entry? _____

   Conference name subject? _____

2. If I search "Shakespeare" in a name browse index, will I find the following?

   `600 10 $aShakespeare, William,$d1564-1616.`

   Yes [ ]   No [ ]

3. If I search "Unesco" in a subject browse index, will I find the following?

   `600 20 $aUnesco.`

   Yes [ ]   No [ ]

4. If I search "Central Intelligence Agency" in a subject keyword index, will I find the following?

   `610 20 $aUnited States.$bCentral Intelligence Agency$xHistory`

   Yes [ ]   No [ ]

Notes

1. Library catalog searches are not normally case-sensitive; a search for "LEWIS, C. S. CLIVE STAPLES" should retrieve the same results as our search for "lewis, c. s. clive staples."

2. Although correct punctuation is important in cataloging, we feel that further discussion of it here would be inappropriate at this introductory level.

3. The *List of Ambiguous Headings* is located at various places on the Web, e.g.:

http://www.oclc.org/western/news/oct01/oct01_ambiguousheadings_cts.htm

http://library.queensu.ca/techserv/cat/Sect05/Auth/ambig.html

4. Perhaps you are wondering why, if indicator 1 has only one value, it is defined at all. This is done because indicator 1 previously had two other values defined (0 and 1), but they have recently become obsolete (something that was once valid practice in the past, but is not valid when creating new records). By making values obsolete, as opposed to invalid, the MARC administrators permit records that were created using previous coding practices to remain viable even after the MARC coding rules have changed.

8

Display Fields—
Bibliographic Description

Let's now look at coding for the display fields, the fields that patrons see. Some of these fields are also indexed and so are searchable. We are not going to cover all the display fields here, just the most common ones.

Title and Statement of Responsibility Area   245

Field 245 (see table 8-1) contains the **title proper** (subfields an$p) and **subtitles** (subfield $b) of a work, as given on the title page of a book, the title screen of a video, the labels of a sound disc, etc. This field also contains:

> a **GMD** (a *general* term describing the type of material) to quickly tell catalog users when the material being described is *not* a book (subfield $h)
>
> a **statement of responsibility** for the intellectual or artistic content of the work (subfield $c)

We index titles as well as display them, and the indicators in this field are very important for indexing.

245 Indicator 1 (Tracing/Indexing Indicator)

Tracing indicators tell the system whether or not to index a field, so the first indicator of the 245 field is *very* important. The intent of this indicator is to tell the system whether or not to index the 245 field. It is admittedly rare that you would not want to allow patrons to search by the title of a work. However, the cataloging

Table 8-1 ■ 245 Coding

245	Title and statement of responsibility
Rule	AACR 1.1
Repeatable	No
Indicator 1	Tracing/Indexing indicator
0	Do not index the title as an added entry
1	Index the title as an added entry
Indicator 2	Filing indicator
0–9	Number of characters to skip before beginning indexing
Subfields	
$a	Title proper
$n	Numbered part or section
$p	Named part or section
$h	General Material Designation (GMD)
$b	Parallel title(s): Other title(s)/subtitle(s); Subsequent title(s) (multiple titles, without a collective title)
$c	Statement of responsibility

rules (AACR2) do specify certain situations when titles should not be indexed, and we use 245 I1 to accomplish this. You will need to concentrate hard here, because this can be a very tricky concept to grasp. Let's see how you do.

245 Indicator 1 = 1 (Index the Title as an Added Entry)

We discussed main entry versus added entries when we covered headings earlier. Remember that:

> if a personal author (100), corporate author (110), conference author (111), or uniform title (130) is present in the record as a main entry, then the title is not the *main* entry; and

> if the title is not the main entry, then it is not automatically indexed; so

> if you want a title that is not a main entry to be indexed, then you need a title *added* entry (so set 245 indicator 1 to 1).

For example, a title browse search on "life is fun" (see fig. 8-1) will find that title in MARC field 245:

```
100 1  $aCarlson, Nancy L.
245 10 $aLife is fun /$cby Nancy Carlson.
```

Because there is a main entry (100) in this example, we need the first indicator in the 245 to be 1 to tell the system to "index the title as an *added entry*" if we want that title to be indexed.

If, instead, we entered a zero in the first indicator in this example, then a search on that title would result in no hits, because this is how we tell the system *not* to index a particular title.

Fig. 8-1 ■ A Title Browse Hitlist for 245 Indicator 1 = 1 at LC

Database Name: Library of Congress Online Catalog
YOU SEARCHED: Title = life is fun
SEARCH RESULTS: Displaying 1 through 4 of 4.

◀ Previous   Next ▶

#	Title	Name: Main Author, Creator, etc.	Full Title	Date
☐ 1	Life is fun /	Carlson, Nancy L.	Life is fun / by Nancy Carlson.	1993

245 Indicator 1 = 0 (Do Not Index the Title as an Added Entry)

On the other hand:

if a personal author (100), corporate author (110), conference author (111), or uniform title (130) is *not* present in a record as a main entry, then the title proper (245) is the main entry; and

main entries are automatically indexed; therefore,

if the title is the *main* entry, then it is automatically indexed and you do not need a title *added* entry (so set 245 indicator 1 to 0).

For example, a title browse search on "careers in focus" (see fig. 8-2) will find records with the title in MARC field 245:

Fig. 8-2 ■ A Title Browse Hitlist for 245 Indicator 1 = 0 at LC

Database Name: Library of Congress Online Catalog
YOU SEARCHED: Title = careers in focus
SEARCH RESULTS: Displaying 1 through 25 of 56.

◀ Previous   Next ▶

#	Title	Name: Main Author, Creator, etc.	Full Title	Date
☐ 1	Careers in focus		Careers in focus. Biology.	2002
☐ 2	Careers in focus		Careers in focus. Social work.	2002
☐ 3	Careers in focus. Agriculture.		Careers in focus. Agriculture.	2001

```
245 00 $aCareers in focus.$pBiology.
```

```
245 00 $aCareers in focus.$pEnergy.
```

```
245 00 $aCareers in focus.$pSocial work.
```

None of these records has an author or a uniform title main entry (1XX). Therefore, even though the first indicator in each of these records is telling the system "do not index the title as an added entry," these titles will be indexed, because in each case the title is the *main* entry, which is automatically indexed.

245 Indicator 2 (Filing Indicator)

In library catalogs, we do not normally file titles under initial articles (introductory words at the beginning of titles, such as "The," "An," "A," "Los," "Las," "El"). If a title begins with an initial article and you do not want to file (index) the title under that article, then you have to tell the system how many characters to skip before beginning filing (indexing).

We skip initial articles in all languages, but we do not skip initial articles that begin proper names (e.g., Los Angeles, Las Vegas, La Toya, El Cid).

Here are a few examples of initial articles and their corresponding indicator 2 values. A complete list of initial articles is given in appendix C and can also be found at LC's MARC website (*Initial Definite and Indefinite Articles* 2000).

```
245 14 $aThe happy Hockey family       (skip 4)
```

```
245 13 $aAn apple a day                (skip 3)
```

```
245 12 $aA day at the races            (skip 2)
```

```
245 10 $aA is for Apple           (do not skip, integral part of title)
```

```
245 14 $aLas casas de mi madre         (skip 4)
```

```
245 10 $aLas Vegas                (do not skip, proper name)
```

Note that even if the title is based on one language and the work is written in another (such as for a translation), we skip the initial article for the language of the title, not the language of the work. For example:

```
245 14 $aLes miserables                (skip 4)
```

However, if we believe that a patron might search for this title under "Les," then we can add another field to provide access by that initial article (see field 246 later in this chapter).

Now let's take a look at how much of a problem incorrect filing indicators can cause in an OPAC. For example, let us do a title browse search on "The" in the LC catalog (see fig. 8-3). This search takes a long time to complete and finds a *huge* number of hits. One of the titles retrieved by this search is:

Fig. 8-3 ■ A Title Browse Hitlist for "The" at LC

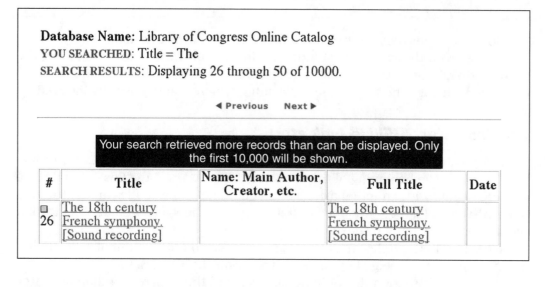

Database Name: Library of Congress Online Catalog
YOU SEARCHED: Title = The
SEARCH RESULTS: Displaying 26 through 50 of 10000.

◀ Previous   Next ▶

Your search retrieved more records than can be displayed. Only the first 10,000 will be shown.

#	Title	Name: Main Author, Creator, etc.	Full Title	Date
☐ 26	The 18th century French symphony. [Sound recording]		The 18th century French symphony. [Sound recording]	

```
245 00 $aThe 18th century French symphony$h[Sound recording].
```

Note the second indicator. The problem here is that the cataloger did not tell the system to skip the first four characters of the title before beginning to index it, so the title was filed under "The." If what we have been telling you is correct, this means that a search on that title, done as it should be without the "The," will not find a match, and sure enough, it does not (see fig. 8-4).

This is a prime example of how items can become "lost" in a catalog. Try a search on "The" in your own catalog and see how many titles such a search finds. Perhaps you will need to organize a cleanup project to fix all those bad indicators.[1]

Fig. 8-4 ■ A Title Browse Search without "The" at LC

Database Name: Library of Congress Online Catalog
Your search found no results.
Refer to search examples, check spelling and punctuation, or try another type of search.
Note: Limits are only available for Title and Serial Title searches.

Search by:

○ Subject Browse ○ Name Browse ● Title ○ Serial Title ○ Call Number Browse

Enter search in box (see search examples):

| 18th century french symphony |

[Search] [Reset]

245 Subfields

Now that you understand the importance of the indicators in the 245 field, let us consider how and why fields, such as the 245 field, are broken down into subfields.

Figure 8-5 shows how LC displays a title in a full record display, and following that is the title coded in MARC:

Fig. 8-5 ■ An LC Full Record Display of a Title

| Brief Record | Subjects/Content | Full Record | MARC Tags |

The fabulous Fantoras. by Adèle Geras ; illustrated by Eric Brace.

LC Control Number: 98053344
Type of Material: Book (Print, Microform, Electronic, etc.)
Personal Name: Geras, Adèle.
Main Title: The fabulous Fantoras. Book two, Family photographs / by Adèle Geras ; illustrated by Eric Brace.

```
245 14 $aThe fabulous Fantoras.$nBook two,$pFamily photographs /$cby Adèle
       Geras ; illustrated by Eric Brace.
```

There are four subfields in the 245 of our preceding example:

Subfield $a—Title proper (is indexed in: title browse and title keyword)

Subfield $n—Numbered part or section (is indexed in: title browse and title keyword)

Subfield $p—Named part or section (is indexed in: title browse and title keyword)

Subfield $c—Statement of responsibility (is indexed in: name keyword)

One reason for splitting fields into subfields is to aid in indexing. We can instruct the system to index different subfields in different contexts (i.e., as a name, as a subject, as a title). In most systems, we want to index subfields anpb (see "subfield $b" later in this chapter) in the title index (browse and keyword), and subfield $c (the statement of responsibility) in the name keyword index. We could not make this distinction if MARC did not provide subfields.

Just as subfields allow us finer control of indexing, they also provide a means for finer control of display. In a full record display, showing the subfield $c is desirable; but in a brief record or hitlist display, the opposite is true: we do not have enough space on these screens to display the often lengthy subfield $c information. So, we can tell our system to display only subfields anpb in areas where we need to be brief (see fig. 8-6).

Fig. 8-6 ■ An LC Title List Display

Database Name: Library of Congress Online Catalog
YOU SEARCHED: Title = fabulous fantoras
SEARCH RESULTS: Displaying 1 through 2 of 2.

◄ Previous   Next ►

#	Title	Name: Main Author, Creator, etc.	Full Title	Date
☐ 1	The fabulous Fantoras. Book one. Family files /	Geras, Adèle.	Fabulous Fantoras. Book one, Family files / by Adèle Geras ; illustrated by Eric Brace.	1998
☐ 2	The fabulous Fantoras. Book two. Family photographs /	Geras, Adèle.	Fabulous Fantoras. Book two, Family photographs / by Adèle Geras ; illustrated by Eric Brace.	1999

Then we can tell the system to display subfields anpb *and* $c where we have more space to show more complete information (refer to fig. 8-5).

So, subfields are important and must be coded correctly in order for the system to handle the MARC data correctly.

Let's look at subfield $h and subfield $b in more detail. Subfield $h is indexed in title browse and title keyword. Subfield $h in MARC field 245 is used to code the GMD (general material designation—what the item *is*). The data that can be entered in subfield $h is tightly controlled by the cataloging rules; currently, only about thirty valid terms can be used as a GMD. A few of the more common examples follow.

MARC displays:

```
245 00 $aJohnny Appleseed$h[videorecording] /$cRabbit Ears Productions ;
       director, C.W. Rogers ; animation, Stan Olson.
```

```
245 00 $aWhere Britain stands$h[sound recording] :$bthe Conservative view
       /$cMargaret Thatcher.
```

```
245 14 $aIn unison 2000$h[text (large print)] :$bpersons with disabilities in
       Canada /$cFederal, Provincial and Territorial Ministers Responsible
       for Social Services.
```

OPAC full record displays:

Title:	Johnny Appleseed [videorecording] / Rabbit Ears Productions ; director, C.W. Rogers ; animation, Stan Olson.

Title:	Where Britain stands [sound recording] : the Conservative view / Margaret Thatcher.

Title:	In unison 2000 [text (large print)] : persons with disabilities in Canada / Federal, Provincial and Territorial Ministers Responsible for Social Services.

We should note that LC does not use the GMD for "large print," but AACR2 (the cataloging rule book) allows it, so you may certainly use it in your local catalog. Finally, note that no GMD exists for the type of material that is still predominant in our catalogs—books:

```
245 00 $aZinn and the art of mountain bike maintenance /$cLennard Zinn ;
       illustrated by Todd Telander.
```

Title:	Zinn and the art of mountain bike maintenance / Lennard Zinn ; illustrated by Todd Telander.

The current cataloging convention is to add only the subfield $h GMD for materials that are *not* books.

Subfield $b is indexed in title browse and title keyword. Subfield $b in MARC field 245 plays a variety of roles. It usually contains other title information, primarily a subtitle, but it can also contain a **parallel title** (needed when an item carries titles in more than one language), or **subsequent title** (needed when an item carries titles for more than one work published within the same physical item). Subfield $b is not repeatable, as you can see from the following examples.

Subfield $b—Other Title/Subtitle:

```
245 10 $aVivaldi :$bvoice of the baroque /$cH.C. Robbins Landon.
```

```
245 00 $aQ :$bquestion : the independent political review.
```

Title:	Vivaldi : voice of the baroque / H.C. Robbins Landon.

Title:	Q : question : the independent political review.

Subfield $b—Parallel Title:

```
245 10 $aWood Cree =$bLes Cris des forets.
```

```
245 00 $aTekstiiliteollisuuden vuosikirja =$bTextilindustrins arsbok = The
       textile industry yearbook.
```

Title:	Wood Cree = Les Cris des forets.

Title:	Tekstiiliteollisuuden vuosikirja = Textilindustrins arsbok = The textile industry yearbook.

Subfield $b—Subsequent Titles:

```
245 10 $aFalse scent$h[text (large print)] ;$bScales of justice ; Singing in
       the shrouds /$cby Ngaio Marsh.
```

```
245 00 $aLord Macaulay ;$bThe task of the modern historian ; The Puritans ; The
       trial of Warren Hastings ; Dr. Samuel Johnson ; Lord Byron ; England
       under the restoration ; The death of Charles II ; The restoration [!]
       of 1688 ; The origin of the national debt.
```

Title:	False scent [text (large print)] ; Scales of justice ; Singing in the shrouds / by Ngaio Marsh.

Title:	Lord Macaulay ; The task of the modern historian ; The Puritans ; The trial of Warren Hastings ; Dr. Samuel Johnson ; Lord Byron ; England under the restoration ; The death of Charles II ; The restoration [!] of 1688 ; The origin of the national debt.

Variant Title   246

The 246 field (see table 8-2) is used to enter other titles that are found on the item but could not be given in the 245 field (e.g., titles found on the spine or cover or container, etc.). Field 246 also contains variations of spelling, etc., for the words given in the title proper in the 245 field. The 246 is very useful when a patron might want to search by one of these unofficial titles.[2] We index this **variant title** field as well as display it, and the indicators in this field are very important both for indexing and for displaying.

Table 8-2 ■ 246 Coding

246	Variant title
Rule	AACR 1.7B4, 1.7B5, 21.30J
Repeatable	Yes
Indicator 1	Display/indexing specifications
0	Display, but do not index
1	Display and index
2	Do not display, and do not index
3	Do not display, but index
Indicator 2	Display constants
#	No display constant—Use with $i, or for alternative titles
0	No display constant—Portion of title (e.g., part or subtitle)
1	No display constant—Parallel title
2	Distinctive title:
3	Other title:
4	Cover title:
5	Added title page title:
6	Caption title:
7	Running title:
8	Spine title:
Subfields	
$i	Display text:
$a	Title
$n	Numbered part or section
$p	Named part or section
$b	Remainder of title

246 Indicator 1—Display/Indexing Specifications

Indicator 1 tells the system whether or not to display the field, and whether or not to index it. If you are unable to find an item in your database by a variant title, even though that variant title was entered in the MARC record, indicator 1 is the culprit; similarly, if a variant title is not displayed in the full record view, but is present in the MARC record, then again, you should immediately suspect that this indicator was entered incorrectly.

If we want patrons to be able to search by a variant title, then we must set indicator 1 in the 246 field to either 1 or 3. The most common coding you will see is indicator 1 set to 3 (index the field, but do not display it):

```
245 10 $aSlaughterhouse-five
246 3  $aSlaughter house five
```

The 246 in the preceding example is simply providing access through a variant spelling of the title in the 245. Therefore, because we will display the 245, there is no need to also display the 246 in the OPAC:

Title:	Slaughterhouse-five

Next, we have an example in which the cataloger is trying to imagine alternate ways that a patron might search for a title:

```
245 14 $aThe complete idiot's guide to trouble-free home repair /$cby David J.
        Tenenbaum.
246 30 $aIdiot's guide to trouble-free home repair
```

The cataloger has entered this variant title thinking that a patron might be more likely to search by "idiot's guide" than by "complete idiot's guide." The first indicator is coded 3 (index, but do not display) because the variant title is already part of the title proper, so there is no need to display it again separately. If we were to enter 1 instead of 3, then we would be telling the system to both index and display the field:

```
245 14 $aThe complete idiot's guide to trouble-free home repair /$cby David J.
        Tenenbaum.
246 10 $aIdiot's guide to trouble-free home repair
```

Here's how this example would look if we were to show both the title and the variant title in the OPAC display:

Title:	The complete idiot's guide to trouble-free home repair / by David J. Tenenbaum.
Variant title:	Idiot's guide to trouble-free home repair

Do we really need to display the variant title? Won't the patron who searches under "idiot's guide" understand how she got to this record if we set the 246 first indicator to 3 and just show her the title and subtitle from the 245?

Title:	The complete idiot's guide to trouble-free home repair / by David J. Tenenbaum.

Sometimes, however, we *do* need to display the 246 to explain where we got it from. Remember, we do not ever want a patron to get to a record and not see the search term that got her there. We will see examples of how we do this with a first indicator set to 1 in the next section on indicator 2.

Indicator 1 is coded 0 (display the variant title, but do not index it) when we are simply adding descriptive information to the record and do not need an additional heading for that information:

```
245 10 $aHigh-performance soccer /$cPaul Caligiuri with Dan Herbst.
246 0  $iSubtitle on cover:$aTechniques & tactics for advanced play
```

The information added from the book cover in the preceding example is informative and descriptive, so we want to display it to patrons, but we do not believe any patron is likely to search by it.

You should not find any 246 fields with the second indicator coded 2, because this tells the system to neither display the variant title nor index it, and we can't imagine when anyone would ever want to do that.

246 Indicator 2—Display Constants

The 246 second indicator tells the system how the cataloger devised the title entered in the 246. Values 2–8 for this indicator should produce display constants. A *display constant* is a label or helpful piece of information that the system is supposed to automatically insert before a MARC field when it displays the record.

In the following example, indicator 1 in the 246 = 1 (display *and* index the field), and indicator 2 in the 246 = 4:

```
245 04 $aThe Berlitz travellers guide to San Francisco & Northern California.
246 14 $aSan Francisco & Northern California
```

The 4 will generate the display constant "cover title:" when the field is displayed in the OPAC:

Title:	The Berlitz travellers guide to San Francisco & Northern California.
Cover title:	San Francisco & Northern California

If none of the display constants that can be produced by I2 are appropriate (see the list in table 8-2), then we enter # (a blank) in I2 instead, and use subfield $i to enter the text we would like to see used as a label:

```
245 10 $aEzra Pound reading$h[sound recording]
246 1  $iTitle on container:$aEzra Pound reading his poetry
```

Title:	Ezra Pound reading [sound recording]
Variant title:	**Title on container:** Ezra Pound reading his poetry

Subfield $i is very useful in the 246 field, because the list of display constants available for indicator 2 values does not cover every eventuality.

We also code the second indicator with a blank when we are simply spelling out abbreviations or numbers, as in an earlier example:

```
245 10 $aSlaughterhouse-five
246 3  $aSlaughter house five
```

Remember that, when I1 = 3, the 246 does not display to patrons. On the other hand, if we want to tell the system (not the patrons) that we got our 246 from a portion of a title or from a parallel title, we use I2 = 0 or 1, respectively.

In the following example, the second indicator tells the system that we got our variant title from a portion of the 245, in this case the subtitle:

```
245 14 $aThe complete idiot's guide to trouble-free home repair /$cby David J.
        Tenenbaum.
246 30 $aIdiot's guide to trouble-free home repair
```

Again, we do not need to display the variant title, because the patron can see its contents in the title, and we have told the system that we got that variant title from data that is already present in the title field (245).

246 Subfields

The subfields in a 246 field are very similar to those used in a 245, since both fields deal with titles.

Subfield $a—Title Proper is indexed in title browse and title keyword:

```
245 10 $aWood Cree =$bLes Cris des forets.
246 31 $aCris des forets
```

```
Title:          Wood Cree = Les Cris des forets.
```

Notice that this 246 does not display. Its first indicator told the system not to display it, because the patron will see the parallel title in the title field.

Also notice that we drop the initial article, "Les," in the 246, because we do not have a filing indicator to tell the system to skip it.

Subfield $n—Numbered Part or Section is indexed in title browse and title keyword.

Subfield $p—Named Part or Section is indexed in title browse and title keyword:

```
245 00 $aBook of black heroes.$nVolume two,$pGreat women in America.
246 30 $aGreat women in America
246 18 $aArundel's Book of black heroes.$nVolume two,$pGreat women in America
```

In the preceding example, the first 246 does not display (I1 = 3) because the variant title is part of the 245, but the second 246 does display (I1 = 1) with the display constant "Spine title" (I2 = 8):

```
Title:          Book of black heroes. Volume two, Great women in America.
Spine title:    Arundel's Book of black heroes. Volume two, Great women in America
```

Subfield $b—Subtitle is indexed in title browse and title keyword.

Subfield $i—Display Text is not indexed:

```
245 10 $aDire Straits live$h[sound recording].
246 1  $iContainer title:$aAlchemy :$bDire Straits live
```

Title:	Dire Straits live [sound recording].
Container title:	Alchemy : Dire Straits live

You may have wondered why none of the examples of the 246 ends in a period. That's a good question, but all that we can say is that's what the punctuation rules say.

We hope that you can see how important the variant title field (246) is for improving patron access to the materials in your library collection, and how important the coding in this field is for making it work properly in the OPAC, as is all the coding in MARC records.

Edition Area   250

The 250 field (see table 8-3) contains edition statements found on the item, e.g., "1st ed.," or "30th anniversary issue," or "colorized version." It also can contain a statement about responsibility for a particular edition.

Table 8-3 ■ **250 Coding**

250	Edition
Rule	AACR 1.2
Repeatable	No
Indicator 1	Undefined—Blank
Indicator 2	Undefined—Blank
Subfields	
$a	Edition statement
$b	Statement of responsibility

Subfield $a—Edition Statement is not indexed, usually.

Subfield $b—Statement of Responsibility is indexed in name keyword:

```
250     $aNew rev. ed.
```

```
250     $a1st ed.
```

```
250     $aLarge print ed.
```

```
250     $a1993 issue /$btext by Lars Hamberger.
```

```
250     $aCondensed version /$bby Walter D. Glanze.
```

Edition:	New rev. ed.

Edition:	1st ed.

Edition:	Large print ed.

Edition:	1993 issue / text by Lars Hamberger.

Edition:	Condensed version / by Walter D. Glanze.

Imprint Area   260

The 260 field (see table 8-4) contains **imprint** information—data about the publication, distribution, or production of an item.

Some of the data provided here for patrons to see is also coded in the fixed field 008, where it can be used by the system to qualify searches. For example, if you want to find all works in the library published in Russia, the system checks the country code for Russia in the 008, rather than trying to figure out from the 260$a (place of publication) which of the cities listed there are in Russia. We will talk more about coded fields later.

Table 8-4 ■ **260 Coding**

260	Publication details
Rule	AACR 1.4
Repeatable	Yes
Indicator 1	Sequence of publishing statements
#	Not applicable/no info. provided/earliest avail. publisher
2	Intervening publisher
3	Current/latest publisher
Indicator 2	Undefined—Blank
Subfields	
$a	Place of publication
$b	Publisher
$c	Date of publication

Subfield $a—Place of Publication is not indexed; 008 country code is indexed instead.

Subfield $b—Publisher is not indexed, usually.

Subfield $c—Date of Publication is not indexed; 008 date is indexed instead:

```
260     $aNew York :$bViking,$cc1999.
```

Published:	New York : Viking, c1999.

Physical Description Area   300

The 300 field (see table 8-5) contains a physical description of the item being described. Contents of this field will vary substantially depending on the type of material being described.

Table 8-5 ■ 300 Coding

300	Description
Rule	AACR 1.5
Repeatable	Yes
Indicator 1	Undefined—Blank
Indicator 2	Undefined—Blank
Subfields	
$a	Extent of item (for books: pages)
$b	Other physical details (for books: illustrated or not)
$c	Dimensions (for books: height, in centimeters)
$e	Accompanying material

Like the 260, the indicators in the 300 are not defined and none of the subfields are indexed, though they should obviously all be displayed.

The following is an example of a 300 for a book that is accompanied by a sound recording CD:

```
300      $a303 p. :$bill. ;$c23 cm. +$e1 sound disc (digital ; 4 3/4 in.)
```

```
Description:      303 p. : ill. ; 23 cm. + 1 sound disc (digital ; 4 3/4 in.)
```

For a book, the **extent of item** ($a) is the number of pages; "other physical details" ($b) means whether or not the book is illustrated; the "dimensions" ($c) of the item are the height of the book measured in centimeters. Information about "accompanying material" ($e) provides a physical description that is appropriate to the type of material involved.

The following example is a videorecording, without any accompanying material:

```
300      $a2 videocassettes (75 min. ea.) :$bsd., col. ;$c1/2 in.
```

```
Description:      2 videocassettes (75 min. ea.) : sd., col. ; 1/2 in.
```

The extent of item ($a) for a video is the number of physical units and the **SMD** (Specific Material Designation, e.g., videocassette or videodisc) for the video, followed by the running time of the video; other physical details ($b) include whether or not the video has sound and is in color; and the dimensions—which vary according to the type of video ($c)—are, in this example, the width of the videotape given in inches.

The following example is a sound recording, also without accompanying material:

```
300      $a2 sound discs (127 min.) :$bdigital, stereo. ;$c4 3/4 in.
```

```
Description:      2 sound discs (127 min.) : digital, stereo. ; 4 3/4 in.
```

The extent of item ($a) for a sound recording is, again, the number of physical units and the SMD for the sound recording, followed by the playing time of the sound recording; other physical details ($b) include whether the recording is analog or digital, etc.; and the dimensions ($c), which vary according to the type of sound recording—disc, cassette, reel, etc.—are here given as the diameter of the disc measured in inches.

Series Area   4XX

A discussion of MARC, even an introductory one, would be incomplete without going into some detail about series statements. By *series,* catalogers mean "a group of separate items related to one another by the fact that each item bears, in addition to its own title proper [i.e., the MARC 245 field], a collective title applying to the group as a whole" (AACR 1998, glossary, p. 622).

Series are often created by a publisher to group together publications on the same topic or theme, e.g.:

> A Rodale organic gardening book
>
> Everyman's library
>
> What your pet needs
>
> G. K. Hall large print romance series
>
> SUNY series on sport, culture, and social relations
>
> Great lives in brief
>
> Westminster aids to the study of the Scriptures

In the catalog, a series can provide good access to related items. For example, a search on "what your pet needs" would retrieve the following items:

> What your fish needs
>
> What your dog needs
>
> What your cat needs
>
> What your horse needs

Series are not to be confused with a **serial**—a publication issued in successive parts and intended to be issued indefinitely. Serials include everything from academic and professional journals to the popular magazines that appear in your local bookstore and supermarket.

Like the 245 field, a series statement can be considered both a heading and a descriptive field. Unlike the 245 which contains the particular title of *an* item, however, the title of a series can occur on many different items. To group all the different items under one series therefore, the choice of a series title and the way that it is to be entered must be *established* once and always used thereafter for that series. It is this *choice of a series title* that determines which MARC field you will use for the series statement, as we shall now discuss.

Series, Traced   440

The 440 field (see table 8-6) is both indexed and displayed, and contains the title of a series when it is to be indexed as a heading exactly as it appears on the item.

Watch out for the second indicator. It is a filing indicator (as we described for the second indicator of the 245) and so is very important.

Table 8-6 ■ 440 Coding

440	Series, Indexed
Rule	AACR 1.6
Repeatable	Yes
Indicator 1	Undefined—Blank
Indicator 2	Filing indicator
0–9	Nonfiling characters to skip before beginning indexing
Subfields	
$a	Series title
$n	Numbered part or section
$p	Named part or section
$v	Series numbering

440 Subfields

The subfields in a 440 are very similar to those used in a 245 and a 246, since these fields all deal with titles. Because the 440 is a title statement and is also an added entry or a heading, it is indexed in the title index (browse and keyword).

```
440   0  $aWhat your pet needs
```

```
440   4  $aThe cooking secrets of the world.$nThird series,$pCooking with spices
```

```
440   0  $aAdvances in experimental medicine and biology ;$vv. 457
```

Series:	What your pet needs

Series:	The cooking secrets of the world. Third series, Cooking with spices

Series:	Advances in experimental medicine and biology ; v. 457

Series, Untraced or Traced Differently   490

The 490 field (see table 8-7) displays but is not indexed. It contains the title of a series that either is *not indexed as a heading at all,* or is *indexed in a different form* than is given on the item. If the latter, then we enter the series as it appears on the item in the 490 field, and enter the series as we wish it to be indexed in an 8XX field (see chapter 7, Indexed Fields).

The first indicator in this field tells the system (and the cataloger) whether or not to look for an 8XX field:

If the first indicator is 0, then the series title is not to be indexed at all, and we should not bother to look for an 8XX field.

If the first indicator is 1, then the series title is to be indexed in a different form than it is given in the 490 (i.e., how it appears on the item). We need to look for an 8XX field to see how the series is established and, therefore, under what it is indexed.

Table 8-7 ■ 490 Coding

490	Series, not indexed, or indexed differently
Rule	AACR 1.6
Repeatable	Yes
Indicator 1	Tracing/Indexing indicator
0	Series is not indexed
1	Series is indexed differently in an 8XX
Indicator 2	Undefined—Blank
Subfields	
$a	Series title
$v	Series numbering

490 Subfields

Other than the subfield $v, used for volume numbering, the 490 uses only a subfield $a for the series statement. And, because the 490 is a descriptive field only (to show what was on the item), it is not indexed.

The difference between how a series statement is entered in the 490 (which is not indexed) and how it is entered as an indexed heading in an 8XX field is often slight. In the following example, the series title found on the item (the 490) is not indexed—the established heading in the 830 is indexed instead.

```
490 1   $aCollections of the Illinois State Historical Library ;$vv. 20
830 0   $aCollections (Illinois State Historical Library) ;$vv. 20.
```

Series:	Collections of the Illinois State Historical Library ; v. 20
Add. series:	Collections (Illinois State Historical Library) ; v. 20.

The important thing to remember is that this series has been established and is indexed in the 830. Even if other publications in this group are issued with slightly different series statements, they will all be grouped under the same heading—the one given in the 830.

Once in awhile, the series should not be indexed at all:

```
490 0   $aThe Nature Company guides
```

Series:	The Nature Company guides

In the preceding example, the cataloger did not think that this particular series would provide any useful access in the catalog, so he used the 490 alone (to tell the patrons that the item is in this series), and set the first indicator to 0 to turn off indexing for the series.

Note that some libraries decide to play it safe and index 490 fields in the title keyword index, on the odd chance that the untraced 490 will provide access to the item not available from the rest of the record.

Notes Area   5XX

All MARC tags that begin with 5 contain notes that catalogers feel patrons might find useful (see table 8-8). Some of these fields are displayed for informational purposes only and are not indexed. Others are both displayed *and* indexed *in keyword indexes*. You should find out which note fields are indexed in your system.

Table 8-8 ■ 5XX Coding

5XX	Notes
Rule	AACR 1.6
Repeatable	Yes
Indicator 1	Undefined—Blank (unless otherwise noted)
Indicator 2	Undefined—Blank (unless otherwise noted)
Subfields	
$a	Note

Notes are supposed to be entered and displayed in the order specified by the cataloging rules (AACR2), but the order of the MARC tags for notes does not follow this order. Because of this divergence, it is difficult to predict in what order notes will be shown on any given system, much less in any given record.

If a note is general in nature, then it will be given in a 500 field. This means that 500 fields are usually not indexed in systems—they are present for informational display only, not for searching.

However, if the contents of a note field are specialized or require special handling (e.g., they could provide good keyword access), then that note will usually have its own 5XX tag defined for it. Here are a few examples of specialized notes fields that are usually keyword indexed in most systems:

Dissertation note (502): particulars about the degree, institution, and date of a thesis

Contents note (505): a list of the titles of the works in a collection, or the table of contents of an item

Credits note (508): names of persons who participated in the production of a work

Performer note (511): names of performers, players, narrators, etc. involved in a work

Summary note (520): a summary, a review, or an abstract of the contents of a work

Most notes do not define any indicators, and most notes you will see make use of $a only. We are going to look at the contents note (505) in detail to illustrate the type of contents that can be found in notes as well as some interesting coding. For the meaning of other note fields, see a MARC manual (*MARC Concise 1999*).

Formatted Contents Note   505

The 505 field (see table 8-9) contains the titles of separate works in a collection, or the table of contents of a work. Indicator 1 dictates which label the system should display for this field.

Table 8-9 ■ 505 Coding

505	Contents
Rule	AACR 1.6
Repeatable	Yes
Indicator 1	Display constant
0	Contents:
1	Incomplete contents:
2	Partial contents:
Indicator 2	Level of contents
#	Basic
0	Enhanced
Subfields	
$a	Basic contents (no names)
$g	Miscellaneous information (not needing indexing)
$r	Statement of responsibility
$t	Title

505 Subfields

Subfield $a is used for a "basic" 505 (I2 = blank), when all the contents of the note can be indexed in the title keyword index:

```
245 10 $aBusiness as usual$h[sound recording] /$cMen at work.

505 0  $aWho can it be now? -- I can see it in your eyes -- Down under --
          Underground -- Helpless automation -- People just love to play with
          words -- Be good Johnny -- Touching the untouchables -- Catch a star -
          - Down by the sea.
```

In the preceding example, the 505 field contains the playlist from a sound recording, listing the title of each song on the recording. It is appropriate to index all the contents of this note in the title keyword index. Notice that the first indicator (a display constant indicator—remember the 246 tag), is set to 0, so the system displays "Contents" as the label for the note:

Title:	Business as usual [sound recording] / Men at work.
Contents:	Who can it be now? -- I can see it in your eyes -- Down under -- Underground -- Helpless automation -- People just love to play with words -- Be good Johnny -- Touching the untouchables -- Catch a star -- Down by the sea.

Let's look at another playlist that is coded quite differently. When the entire contents of a 505 note should not all be indexed in the title keyword index, we make an enhanced 505 (I2 = 0) instead. Subfield $t is used for titles, subfield $r is used for responsibility, and subfield $g is possibly used for miscellaneous information. This would be the case for a contents note that contains names, titles, and running times, as in the following example:

```
245 00 $aMusic from the court of Frederick the Great$h[sound recording].

505 00 $tTrio sonata in B flat major /$rCarl Philipp Emanuel Bach$g(19:36) --
       $tSonata for violin and basso continuo in A minor /$rFranz
       Benda$g(13:02) --$tSonata for flute in C minor /$rFrederick the
       Great$g(8:29) --$tHarpsichord sonata in A major H186 /$rCarl Philipp
       Emanuel Bach$g(15:55) --$tTrio sonata in G minor /$rJohann Gottlieb
       Graun$g(9:37) --$tConcerto for flute in A major /$rJohann Joachim
       Quantz$g(12:06).
```

When both names and titles are present in a contents note, such as in a compilation recording like this one, we separate the names from the titles using subfield $r (for name) and subfield $t (for title); this way, the names can be indexed in the name keyword index, and the titles can be indexed in the title keyword index. Subfield $g is also useful in this regard, because data entered here will display but will not be indexed:

Contents:	Trio sonata in B flat major / Carl Philipp Emanuel Bach (19:36) -- Sonata for violin and basso continuo in A minor / Franz Benda (13:02) -- Sonata for flute in C minor / Frederick the Great (8:29) -- Harpsichord sonata in A major H186 / Carl Philipp Emanuel Bach (15:55) -- Trio sonata in G minor / Johann Gottlieb Graun (9:37) -- Concerto for flute in A major / Johann Joachim Quantz (12:06).

Here again, notice that the first indicator is coded 0, so the system displays "Contents" as the label for the note. If the cataloger is unable to list all the contents of a work, perhaps because of space constraints, indicator 1 would be coded 2, and the system would display "Partial contents" as the label for the note instead.

The other possibility for tag 505 indicator 1 is 1, for "Incomplete contents," which is used when an item has multiple volumes; contents are provided for all the volumes that are currently available, but the indicator is coded 1 to show that additional contents (volumes) may become available and be added to the note later.

Also consider that a 505 field can get rather lengthy—imagine how long it would be for a collection of ten or more CD-ROMs on the history of a musical genre, such as opera or the blues. However, MARC is flexible enough to accommodate fields of various sizes, from one byte to many, many thousands.[3]

QUIZ 8

1. If I search "Saint vs. Scotland Yard" in a title browse index, will I find the following?

```
100 1  $aCharteris, Leslie,$d1907-
245 04 $aThe Saint vs. Scotland Yard
```

Yes [ ]   No [ ]

2. If I search "Saint vs. Scotland Yard" in a title browse index, will I find the following?

```
100 1  $aCharteris, Leslie,$d1907-
245 10 $aThe Saint vs. Scotland Yard
```

Yes [　]　　No [　]

3. If I search "Utopian adventure" in a title browse index, will I find the following?

```
245 10 $aSpending :$ba utopian divertimento /$cMary Gordon.
246 02 $aA utopian adventure
```

Yes [　]　　No [　]

4. If I search "Copeland studies" in a title browse index, will I find the following?

```
100 1  $aTebeau, Charlton W.
245 10 $aMan in the Everglades.
440  0 $aCopeland studies in Florida history ;$vno. 3
```

Yes [　]　　No [　]

5. If I search "chronicles of Narnia" in a title browse index, will I find the following?

```
100 1  $aLewis, C. S. $q(Clive Staples),$d1898-1963.
245 10 $aThe Lion, the witch and the wardrobe.
490 0  $aThe chronicles of Narnia
```

Yes [　]　　No [　]

Notes

1. If, at some later date, you are unable to reproduce this example in the LC catalog, it may mean that LC has finally organized a project to fix all its filing indicators. Also, be aware that some OPACs have "smart" options to deal with nonfiling indicators, either on the user end (if the patron enters "the cat in a hat," the search engine removes "the"), or on the indexing end (the system recognizes common initial articles even if the nonfiling indicators are wrongly coded). These solutions can cause some interesting search problems of their own, however, which you might want to investigate further. Whatever your current OPAC options might provide as a workaround, we recommend that, for best results, you rely on correct coding of this 245 indicator and not on any such "smart" options.

2. Catalogers are instructed to take the official title for a record, the title proper (MARC 245), from something called the "chief source of information," which, for a book, is the title page.

3. How big can a MARC field be? The maximum length for a MARC *field* is 9,999 bytes, and the maximum length for a MARC *record* is 99,999 bytes. Because most MARC records are less than 3,000 bytes, this leaves a lot of space for contents notes, although some may have to be split into more than one 505 field, which is fine, because the 505 is repeatable.

9

Coded Fields

Except for the 001 and 005 tags, all tags that begin with 00 are for coded fields (also called *control fields*). They are called *coded fields* because these fields contain only short codes obtained from various lookup lists. Because a discussion of coded fields is a hefty topic in its own right, we are going to focus more on how these coded fields work than on the various codes involved.[1]

In the first place, the coded fields are for the use of the computer, not patrons. By this we mean that although (some) coded fields are sometimes indexed (in a way), they are never displayed to patrons. The primary use of coded fields is to provide a way to limit, qualify, or narrow searches that retrieve too many hits in a catalog.

Let's look at the **search limits** screen from the LC catalog (see fig. 9-1). Except the collection location, which comes from the holdings information, the data for all these search limiters or qualifiers comes from either the 000 or the 008 field (see table 9-1).

Fields 006 and 007 also contain codes that could be used for limiting searches. But since most library automation systems currently recognize only a few codes from the 000 and the 008, and rarely use codes from the 006 and 007 (yet), we are going to concentrate on explaining the 000 and 008 codes. Let's have a brief look at them.

Leader   000

The 000 field is more properly called the "leader."[2] It is a string of twenty-four bytes of data that appears at the beginning of every MARC record. The leader is not really a field in the same sense that all the other MARC tags are fields. It is a

Fig. 9-1 ■ The Search Limits Menu at LC

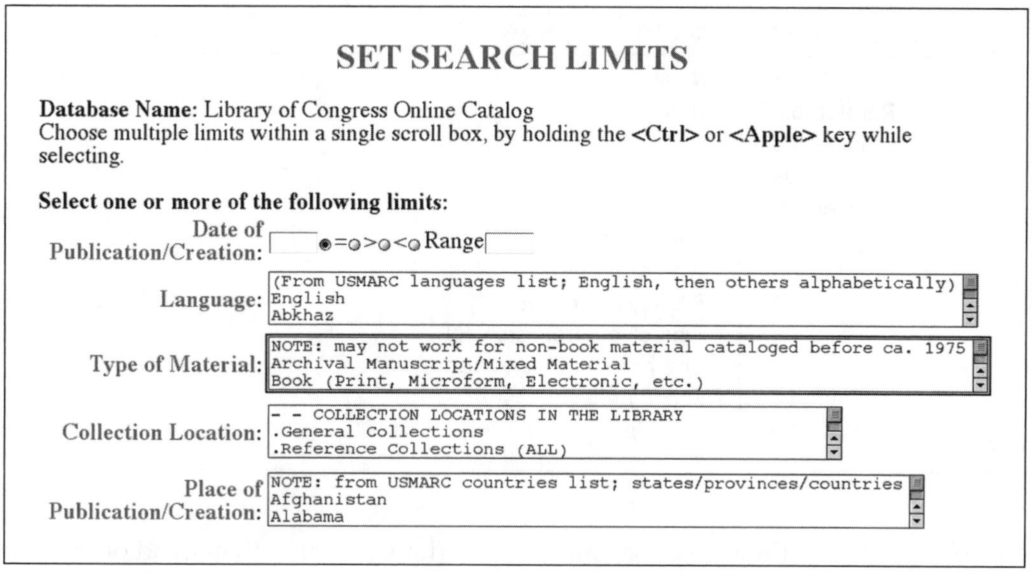

SET SEARCH LIMITS

Database Name: Library of Congress Online Catalog
Choose multiple limits within a single scroll box, by holding the <Ctrl> or <Apple> key while selecting.

Select one or more of the following limits:

Date of
Publication/Creation: ⬚ ⦿=○ >○ <○ Range ⬚

Language:
```
(From USMARC languages list; English, then others alphabetically)
English
Abkhaz
```

Type of Material:
```
NOTE: may not work for non-book material cataloged before ca. 1975
Archival Manuscript/Mixed Material
Book (Print, Microform, Electronic, etc.)
```

Collection Location:
```
- - COLLECTION LOCATIONS IN THE LIBRARY
.General Collections
.Reference Collections (ALL)
```

Place of
Publication/Creation:
```
NOTE: from USMARC countries list; states/provinces/countries
Afghanistan
Alabama
```

Table 9-1 ■ Qualifier Coding

Qualifier	MARC field
Date of publication:	008 Date1
Language:	008 Lang
Type of material:	000 Type of record
Place of publication/creation:	008 Ctry

part of the header, or control information, in the raw MARC record. Here is how the leader looks in most MARC record displays:

```
000  00876nam  2200277 a 4500
```

The leader contains coded information that tells the system important facts about the MARC *record* itself, rather than about the material being described (see table 9-2). Because the leader is not a variable field, the concepts of repeatability, indicators, and subfields do not apply.

When we are referring to the "elements" or "components" or "parts" of a coded or control field, we usually just give the name of the element, or an abbreviation of it. Some examples in cataloger-speak are: "record status" or "rec stat," "record type" or "rec type," "bib level" or "bibliographic level," etc., rather than "leader rec stat," etc.

The numbers in the column on the right in table 9-2 indicate the position of each element in the leader. Some catalogers (and most programmers) refer to

Table 9-2 ■ Leader Coding

000	Leader
AACR	None
Repeatable	N/A
Indicators	N/A
Subfields	N/A
Codes are given for	
05	Record status
06	Type of record
07	Bibliographic level
08	Type of control (archival)
17	Character coding scheme
18	Encoding level
19	Descriptive cataloging form

these elements by their position, such as: "leader six" (000/06) instead of "record type."[3] We think it is easier to use the name instead of the number when referring to these elements.

Most systems can use the "type of record" code from the leader to qualify searches by type of material, and since this code can have a great impact on access, it is worth going into detail about it. Table 9-3 shows the current list of valid

Table 9-3 ■ Type of Record Coding

000/06	Type of record
a	language material (e.g., a book)
t	manuscript language material (e.g., theses, letters)
g	projected medium (e.g., videos, filmstrips, slides)
k	two-dimensional, nonprojected graphics (e.g., photos)
r	3-D artifact or natural object (e.g., sculpture, equipment)
o	kit
i	sound recording, nonmusical (e.g., a book on tape)
j	sound recording, musical (e.g., opera on a CD)
m	electronic resource (e.g., software)
c	music printed (e.g., scores, songbooks)
d	music manuscript
e	map, printed (e.g., travel maps, atlases)
f	map, manuscript
p	mixed material (archival)

codes that may be entered into the record type position in the leader for a bibliographic record. The most common code for type of record is "a" for books and other print materials. To find the record type code in the following example, you would count over to the record type position (06), remembering to begin counting at 0, not 1:

```
000        00876nam  2200277 a 4500
position 01234567
```

Catalogers must be careful that the record type position is coded correctly for all types of materials. Let's say that we are searching for nonmusical sound recordings of *Hamlet* in the LC OPAC. An "unqualified" search for "Hamlet" in the LC OPAC will retrieve over 2,300 hits, so we want to narrow, or "qualify," our search by type of material (see fig. 9-2). When we do our search with this limit turned on, we retrieve only thirty-six hits instead. That's a big difference!

Fig. 9-2 ■ The Type of Material Search Limit at LC

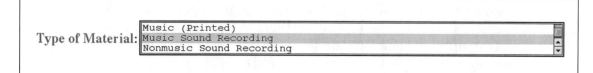

However, a record for a nonmusical sound recording would not be retrieved by this qualified search if that record was coded "a" instead of "i" in the record type position. That record would, in effect, be lost, because a patron is not likely to browse through all 2,300 hits on "Hamlet" to stumble across the desired sound recording record.

We hope you can see that the record type code is very important. In addition, your system will use this code when it generates statistics on how many records you have in your collection for each type of material.

Another important leader code is the one for bibliographic level. The code "m," for example, means that the record is for a **monograph;** the code "s" means that the record is for a serial.

The following is another example of a MARC display for a leader. This is the leader for a record that describes some type of projected material (type of record code: g):

```
000 00876cgm  2200277I 4500
```

A separate code is used to tell the system whether the projected material is a videorecording, motion picture, slide, transparency, filmstrip, etc., and that code is found in the 008 field, which we will go to now.

By the way, OCLC combines leader codes with 008 codes in its display, and we will look at an OCLC display of this field at the end of our coverage of the 008.

Fixed-Length Data Elements   008

The 008 field is often called the **fixed field** because it always contains forty bytes of data. The 008 contains coded information that tells a system details about both *the record* and *the material being described by the record* (see table 9-4). Note that the 008 field, like all the other control fields, is nonrepeatable and has no indicators or subfields.

Table 9-4 ▪ 008 Coding

008	Fixed-length data elements
AACR	None
Repeatable	No
Indicators	None
Subfields	None

Most OPACs will use the codes entered in the 008 to allow a patron to qualify searches by language (e.g., everything in the collection by Shakespeare in Spanish), or by publication date (e.g., everything in the collection on space exploration published between 1963 and 1969).

However, catalogers code a great deal more than just language and date of publication in the 008. For example:

> the place of publication or production
>
> whether a book is illustrated, or has maps, portraits, etc.
>
> the intended audience (juvenile, young adult, unspecified) of an item
>
> whether a book is in large print or braille
>
> whether a sound recording is folk music, jazz, blues, etc.
>
> the running time of a video or motion picture
>
> the frequency of publication for a serial

It is unfortunate, but most systems do not make this additional coded information searchable in the OPAC, although LC's system does include the place of publication in its qualifier options.

One of the things about the 008 field that makes it so difficult to learn is the way that it varies depending on the record type code (which we looked at in the leader). If a record type is coded "a" for print material, then nineteen elements are defined for the 008; but if the record type is coded "m" for electronic resource, then only fifteen elements are defined in the 008.

However, eight elements in the 008 are always defined the same way for all types of materials (see table 9-5). These elements are found in all MARC bibliographic records. Note that, like the components of a leader, these elements are identified by their position in the field (starting at zero); if a code for an element is longer than one character, its starting and ending positions are indicated.[4]

Table 9-5 ■ 008 Coding for All Types of Materials

008	Fixed-length data elements
00–05	Date record added to database
06	Date type or publication status
07–10	Date 1
11–14	Date 2
15–17	Place of publication or production (uses the code list for countries; e.g., nyu for New York State)
35–37	Language (uses the code list for languages; e.g., eng for English)
38	Modified record code
39	Cataloging source

Here is a typical MARC display for field 008:

```
008      870807s1986    nyua   g     000 0 eng
```

From this example and table 9-5, once we learn how to read the 008, we can see that this MARC record was created on August 7, 1987 (870807), that only one date is provided in the 008 (s), that the book being described was published in 1986 in New York State (nyu), that it is written in English (eng), that the record was not modified when it was entered (blank), and that a national bibliographic agency (e.g., LC) is the source of cataloging for the record (blank).

We also know, from the codes shown in this 008, that this book is illustrated (a), intended for a general audience (g), not a reproduction (blank), not an abstract, a dictionary, or one of the other types of works on the contents code list (blank), not a government publication (blank), not a conference publication (0), and not a **festschrift** (0). It also has no index (0) and is nonfiction (0). We will discuss some of these other codes in more detail shortly. We will also look at a more user-friendly display for the 008.

As we said earlier, almost all online library catalogs can limit or qualify searches by date of publication, which contains a four-digit year, e.g., 1993, 1994, and 2001, and by language, which contains a three-character code, such as eng (English), fre (French), and spa (Spanish). A few systems, such as the one at LC, can also limit a search by the place of publication (in our example, nyu—New York).

Another important thing to know is that because these elements are coded, the cataloger cannot enter just any old thing into the 008. The codes that may be entered in the 008 elements must be taken from various lists and tables in the MARC manual. For example, figure 9-3 shows the beginning of the controlled list of codes for the place of publication, and figure 9-4 shows the beginning of the controlled list of codes for the language element.

Now let's briefly look at the 008 elements that differ depending on the type of material that is described by the record. For example, table 9-6 lists the elements that are required for print material (e.g., a book—leader record type = a).

Fig. 9-3 ■ The MARC21 Code List for Countries

MARC Country Codes

Part II: Code Sequence

Discontinued codes are identified by a hyphen preceding the code

aa Albania
abc Alberta
-ac Ashmore and Cartier Islands
ae Algeria
af Afghanistan
ag Argentina
-ai Anguilla
ai Armenia (Republic)
-air Armenian S.S.R.
aj Azerbaijan

Fig. 9-4 ■ The MARC21 Code List for Languages

MARC Language Codes

Part II: Code Sequence

NOTE: Discontinued codes are also listed in this sequence. They are identified by a hyphen preceding the code.

CODE LIST

aar Afar
abk Abkhaz
ace Achinese
ach Acoli
ada Adangme
afa Afroasiatic (Other)
afh Afrihili (Artificial language)
afr Afrikaans

Table 9-6 ◼ 008 Coding for Books

Position	Element
18–21	Illustrations
22	Target audience
23	Form of item
24–27	Nature of contents
28	Government publication
29	Conference publication
30	Festschrift
31	Index
32	Undefined—Blank
33	Literary form
34	Biography

Each element defined in table 9-6, of course, has a list of valid codes that can be entered in that position of the 008 field. For example, table 9-7 lists the valid codes that can be used for an 008 for a book, in position 22 (target audience). So, a book that is written for elementary-school readers should have a "c" coded in position 22 (target audience), whereas a book intended for young adults would be coded "d."

We hope you can see just how valuable it is for you to have this type of coding provided correctly in your MARC records, even if it is only for collection analysis and statistics. Perhaps someday all systems will make all of these codes available for enhanced searching.

Table 9-7 ◼ 008 Target Audience Coding

Code	Meaning
#	Unknown or not specified
a	Preschool
b	Primary
c	Elementary
d	Secondary
e	Adult
f	Specialized
g	General
j	Juvenile
l	No attempt to code

Getting back to the MARC display of coded fields, figure 9-5 shows a typical labeled display for an 008. Note how the labels make it somewhat easier to read the field.

Fig. 9-5 ■ A Generic Display of the Marc 008 Field

```
008      760831t19771976jm a      db      001 0 eng

Entrd: 760831      DtSt: t  Dates: 1977,1976      Ctry: jm  Ills: a
Audn:      Form: d  Cont: b  GPub:      Conf: 0  Fest: 0
Indx: 1  M/E:      LitF: 0  Biog:      Lang: eng  MRec:      Srce:
```

Figure 9-6 shows how OCLC displays the same 008. OCLC also includes the elements (that it considers important) from the leader (000) in this display. OCLC has taken all the fixed field codes from the leader and the 008, labeled them, rearranged their order, and put them together in one display.

Fig. 9-6 ■ An OCLC Display of the MARC Fixed Fields

```
OCLC: 2439444  Rec stat:  c
Entered: 19760831  Replaced: 19960410  Used: 19960402
Type: a  ELvl:      Srce:      Audn:      Ctrl:      Lang: eng
BLvl: m  Form: d  Conf: 0  Biog:      MRec:      Ctry: nyu
         Cont: b  GPub:      LitF: 0  Indx: 0
Desc: i  Ills: a  Fest: 0  DtSt: t  Dates: 1977,1976
```

If you are a cataloger, you will have to learn how to interpret these displays and how to enter these coded fields, and your coding manuals will be well worn. For now, just remember that the leader and 008 codes are *very* important. Collection analysis, statistics, and search qualifiers won't work properly if the leader and 008 codes are not entered properly.

QUIZ 9

1. If I qualify a search by type of material = sound recording, will I find the following?

```
000      00876nam 2200277 a 4500 (Type of record = "a")
245 00 $aSound of music soundtrack$h[sound recording].
300      $a1 sound cassette :$banalog
```

Yes [ ]   No [ ]

2. If I qualify a search by date = 1998, will I find the following?

```
008   Date 1: 1998
260      $aNew York :$bBantam,$c1999.
```

Yes [ ]   No [ ]

3. If I qualify a search by language = Spanish, will I find the following?

```
008   Lang: eng
245 04 $aLos muros de agua.
```

Yes [ ]   No [ ]

4. How many 008s can there be in a MARC record?

_____

Notes

1. We count about 230 pages dedicated solely to coded-field information in the latest MARC21 bibliographic manual from LC, and this does not even include the many lists of codes that are applicable to these fields.

2. The use of 000 to label the leader is a convention, since all the other fields are labeled by tag numbers. We believe it is from this convention that the leader has come to be called the 000 tag, since the MARC21 manual does not actually mention the field by number.

3. The positions in these coded fields always begin counting at zero. So, the first character in the leader is called "position zero"; the second, "position one"; and so on.

4. For example, 07–10 means that the code for date 1 starts at position 07 and ends at position 10, and so is four characters in length (7-8-9-10).

10

Number Fields

We will finish our look at specific groups of MARC fields with the number fields. Number fields can be useful for searching. Sometimes a patron has written down an **ISBN** or even an **LCCN** taken from some source and might want to search by it. Even more importantly, catalogers and systems staff find number fields extremely useful for finding MARC records.

> *Number fields and copy cataloging.* Remember that copy cataloging allows us to find a record made by someone else that exactly matches the item that we have in our hand. We can then use that record instead of having to make one from scratch (original cataloging). One of the easiest ways for catalogers to find matching records is to search by a number field, such as LCCN or ISBN, because these numbers are *supposed* to be unique.

> *Number fields and machine matching.* The number fields are also very important for allowing machines to identify duplicate records **(machine matching),** because these numbers are *supposed* to be unique. When we load records to our databases, we have to have some way for our systems to tell whether we already have those records. And, when we link databases for virtual union catalogs, we want to show only one record to patrons, even when numerous libraries have the same record (this is called **deduping-on-the-fly**). Library systems rely on number fields to detect duplicate records.

We are going to describe number fields 001 + 003, 010, and 020.

Control Number 001

The control number identifies an individual record on a particular system, and so it must be unique to that system. A control number is MARCspeak for an accession number (if you are familiar with that term). For example, here is a record in the database at the Library of Congress:

```
001     99124725
003 DLC
245 00 $aFrommer's irreverent guide to San Francisco.
```

And here is the very same record in the database at OCLC:

```
001 ocm39159649
003 OCoLC
245 00 $aFrommer's irreverent guide to San Francisco.
```

Notice that these two records have completely different numbers in their 001 fields. The uniqueness of the control number is further assisted by the 003 field, which we will discuss in the next section.

Because control numbers are *supposed* to be unique within and between systems, they are often used by systems to machine match records.

As table 10-1 shows, the 001 field is not repeatable (it can occur only once in any MARC record) and has no indicators and no subfields. The 001 is so important that it is one of the few fields that are required to be in *every* MARC record.

Table 10-1 ■ 001 Coding

001	Control number
AACR	None
Repeatable	No
Indicators	None
Subfields	None

Control Number Identifier 003

A control number identifier helps to make the control number in the 001 unique in a multidatabase context by specifying the automated system from which the control number comes. In the preceding LC example, the 003 contains the code DLC, which tells us that the control number in the 001 (99124725) is a Library of Congress control number.[1]

However, the same number (99124725) could conceivably be assigned as a control number to a completely different record in another system. In the following example, the 003 code FMlbTMQ tells us that the control number in the 001 is from the TMQ system:

```
001 99124725
003 FMlbTMQ
245 00 $aFrommer's irreverent guide to San Francisco.
```

If, by some chance, the DLC record and the FMlbTMQ records were both to be loaded into the same file, an automation system should be able to distinguish between these numbers by checking the 003. Given that many systems match records based on the 001, it should be easy for you to now see why it is important to enter and code the 003 correctly in all your records.

Like the 001 field, the 003 field is not repeatable and has no indicators and no subfields (see table 10-2). The control number identifier is another of the fields that are *required* in every MARC record.

Table 10-2 ■ 003 Coding

003	Control number identifier
AACR	None
Repeatable	No
Indicators	None
Subfields	None

Library of Congress Control Number (LCCN)   010

An LCCN, which used to be known as the Library of Congress *Card* Number, identifies a single, specific, individual record in the LC database. Because an LCCN is supposed to be unique, it is often used by systems to machine match records.

The 010 field (see table 10-3) is not repeatable and has two blank indicators. Subfield $a is used for a unique (valid) LCCN. Subfield $z is used for a nonunique (invalid) LCCN and is very important for preventing bad matches, which we explain at the end of this chapter. The formatting of the LCCN in the 010 field has been somewhat complicated by recent developments, but, in general, except on

Table 10-3 ■ 010 Coding

010	LCCN
AACR	1,7B19
Repeatable	No
Indicator 1	Undefined—Blank
Indicator 2	Undefined—Blank
Subfields	
$a	Valid LCCN
$z	Invalid LCCN

OCLC, LC numbers assigned before 2001 should be entered with a prefix of three characters or blank spaces, two digits, no hyphen, and six digits, zero-filled. For example, like this:

```
010      $a   99012345
```

and *not* like this:

```
010      $a99-12345
```

On OCLC, however, the reverse is true, so the LCCN would be entered as 99-12345 there.

From 2001 and on, however, the LCCN should be entered with a prefix of two characters or blank spaces, four digits, no hyphen, and six digits, zero-filled. For example, like this:

```
010      $a   2001012345
```

and *not* like this:

```
010      $a2001-12345
```

Once again on OCLC, however, the reverse is still true, so the LCCN would be entered as 2001-12345 there.[2]

International Standard Book Number (ISBN)   020

An ISBN is intended to identify an individual edition of a publication. Because these numbers are supposed to be unique, they are often used by systems to machine match records.

The 020 field is repeatable (see table 10-4), which means that a MARC record can have more than one 020 field and has two blank indicators. Subfield $a is used for a unique (valid) ISBN. Subfield $z is used for a nonunique (invalid) ISBN and is very important for preventing bad matches, which we explain at the end of this chapter.

Table 10-4 ■ 020 Coding

020	ISBN
AACR	1.8
Repeatable	Yes
Indicator 1	Undefined—Blank
Indicator 2	Undefined—Blank
Subfields	
$a	Valid ISBN
$z	Invalid ISBN
:$c	Terms of availability (e.g., the price of an item)

The ISBN must be entered (on all systems) without any hyphens or blank spaces, like this:

```
020 $a0838907288
```

and *not* like this:

```
020 $a0-8389-0728-8
```

Most catalogers follow LC's lead and no longer use 020 $c. They put price information in a special field in their holdings record instead.

Other Number Fields

Many other fields in MARC records contain numbers, but we are not going to discuss them here, except to point out that classification numbers can be very useful for copy catalogers. There are fields for LC classification numbers (050 or 090), and fields for Dewey classification numbers (082 or 092). These fields contain the classification numbers that were assigned to an item by the library that created the record for the item. You might want to use one of these numbers for your copy of the item, or you might disagree with the other cataloger's choice of numbers and want to assign a completely different number to your item. In any case, these numbers can give you a start on the difficult task of assigning call numbers.

Machine Matching and Bad Matches

Before we leave number fields, we feel it is vital for us to emphasize how very essential the number fields that we have described here are for **duplicate record detection.** If you are a cataloger or systems person, the most important thing that you need to know about number fields is that, as we have mentioned before, some number fields are used for machine matching.

What does your library system do when it adds a new MARC record to the database? Usually the first thing the system attempts to discover is whether the record being added is already present.

When things go as they should, and any of the number fields (001+003, 010, 020) in two MARC records match one another, only one MARC record is kept in the database. The holdings information (barcode number, call number, price, etc.) from one record is added to the MARC record that is retained.

Do the records in figure 10-1 match? Are they the same (other than the 001, the 003, and the 852)? The 001 (control number) and 003 (control number identifier) in these records are different because the first record comes from the Library of Congress database and the second one comes from the OCLC database. The holdings—which, for the sake of this example, we have entered in the 852 subfield $p—show two different barcode numbers, representing two physical copies of the title. Otherwise, these two records are identical.

Even if we have two physical copies of the same item (or two hundred copies), we only need/want one MARC record in the OPAC. So, if we try to load both of these MARC records into the same system, the system should determine

Fig. 10-1 ■ MARC Records Matching Correctly on 010

```
001     83060086
003 DLC
010     $a    83060086
100 1  $aWilliams, Winston.
245 10 $aFlorida's fabulous waterbirds :$btheir stories /$c[by
         Winston Williams].
250     $a3rd ed.
260     $aTampa, FL :$bWorld Publications,$c1987.
300     $a1 v. (unpaged) :$bcol. ill., map ;$c31 cm.
852     $p32424000001239
```

```
001 ocm10215712
003 OCoLC
010     $a    83060086
100 1  $aWilliams, Winston.
245 10 $aFlorida's fabulous waterbirds :$btheir stories /$c[by
         Winston Williams].
250     $a3rd ed.
260     $aTampa, FL :$bWorld Publications,$c1987.
300     $a1 v. (unpaged) :$bcol. ill., map ;$c31 cm.
852     $p32424000001247
```

that they match on the 010 field, and should keep one record and drop the other.[3] This will result in one MARC record describing the title, with two holdings attached, something like the record shown in figure 10-2.

This merging of multiple MARC records into one is a good thing. It prevents duplicate records from being loaded to the system, because duplicate records confuse patrons. It also simplifies system maintenance by preserving a one- (MARC record) -to-many (holdings) relationship.

Sometimes, however, machine matching on number fields does not go as planned, and the system matches records that are not truly identical. This undesired result can happen if the same number is erroneously present in two

Fig. 10-2 ■ MARC Record from Correct Match on 010

```
001     83060086
003 DLC
010     $a    83060086
100 1  $aWilliams, Winston.
245 10 $aFlorida's fabulous waterbirds :$btheir stories /$c[by
         Winston Williams].
250     $a3rd ed.
260     $aTampa, FL :$bWorld Publications,$c1987.
300     $a1 v. (unpaged) :$bcol. ill., map ;$c31 cm.
852     $p32424000001239
852     $p32424000001247
```

completely different records. Because only one MARC record is kept and the holdings from the dropped record are merged to the retained record, we have a problem.

Do the records in figure 10-3 match? In this case, the records are completely different, except for one field. Unfortunately, the one field that is the same in both records, the 020 field, is often a machine-matching field; ergo, these totally different records will match on 020. The result is—since, as we saw, the system will keep only one record in its zeal to cut down on unnecessary duplication—that the holdings from one MARC record will be merged to the other, creating something like the record shown in figure 10-4.

Fig. 10-3 ■ MARC Records Matching Incorrectly on 020

```
001  ocm1735400
003  OCoLC
010      $a   75032250
020      $a0030143667
100 1 $aReed, Bob.
245 10 $aSand creatures and castles :$bhow to build them /$cBob and Pat
         Reed ; illustrated with line drawings and photos.
260      $aNew York :$bHolt, Rinehart and Winston,$cc1976.
300      $a63 p. :$bill. ;$c24 cm.
852      $p32424000005671
```

```
001  ocm2183011
003  OCoLC
010      $a   79087544
020      $a0030143667
100 1 $aWilliams, Barbara.
245 10 $aCornzapoppin'! :$bpopcorn recipes and party ideas for all
         occasions / $cBarbara Williams ; photographs by Royce L. Bair.
260      $aNew York :$bHolt, Rinehart and Winston,$c[1983?] c1976.
300      $a160 p. :$bill. ;$c23 cm.
852      $p32424000005689
```

Fig. 10-4 ■ MARC Record from Incorrect Match on 020

```
001  ocm1735400
010      $a   75032250
020      $a0030143667
100 1 $aReed, Bob.
245 10 $aSand creatures and castles :$bhow to build them /$cBob and
         Pat Reed ; illustrated with line drawings and photos.
260      $aNew York :$bHolt, Rinehart and Winston,$cc1976.
300      $a63 p. :$bill. ;$c24 cm.
852      $p32424000005671
852      $p32424000005689
```

This is called a **bad match,** and yes, it really does happen, not only with the ISBN, but also with the LCCN and with any other number field we have tried to use for matching purposes.

Two problems now exist. First, the record that the system retained, "Sand creatures and castles," now has a barcode attached to it (32424000005689) that doesn't belong there. Second, the MARC record describing the book "Cornzapoppin'" has now completely vanished from the system.

A bad match is often the explanation for why an irate patron insists that she never borrowed the book listed on her overdue notice. The barcode number for the book that was borrowed somehow got attached to a totally different MARC record via the machine match, and the overdue notice simply printed the title to which the barcode was attached. As well as causing a negative effect on community relations, this bad match also means that there is now a book on the shelf (*Cornzapoppin',* if the patron eventually returns it) that is not listed in the database, making the book invisible to patrons using the OPAC.

Bad matches are a bad thing, and we hope that now that you know about them, you will take great care with your number fields and *try* to prevent this from happening. If you ever see the same LCCN or ISBN number in two different records, report it to a cataloger. She will change the subfield code for one of the numbers to $z (invalid) to prevent them matching.

QUIZ 10

1. Must a MARC record have an 001 field?

   Yes [   ]   No [   ]

2. Do 010 fields have indicators?

   Yes [   ]   No [   ]

3. Are number fields important for patrons?

   Yes [   ]   No [   ]

4. Are number fields important for library automation systems?

   Yes [   ]   No [   ]

Notes

1. The codes referred to here can be found in the *MARC Code List for Organizations* (2000), maintained by the Network Development and MARC Standards Office at the Library of Congress.

2. If you want to learn all the gory details, you can read up on the history and structure of the LCCN at http://lcweb.loc.gov/marc/lccn_structure.html.

3. Which record is kept and which record is dropped varies from one system to another. On a good system, you can customize this decision.

11

Summary

In the preceding pages, we have tried to make the following broad points:

- We organize our library materials and provide information about those materials in catalogs. Patrons can search those catalogs and decide from the information provided whether any of our materials meet their educational, informational, and recreational needs. Many library catalogs are now provided on computers instead of on cards, in books, or on microforms.

- We follow specific rules (AACR) for providing bibliographic information and a specific standard for coding that information into a computer record (MARC). Because we follow these rules and standards, libraries can easily share both computer records and library materials.

- MARC was first developed by the Library of Congress in the 1960s and continues to develop and change. The flavor of MARC used in the United States and Canada, and an increasing list of other countries, is MARC21. Different types of MARC21 records contain different types of information; MARC21 bibliographic records contain bibliographic information. Most libraries copy MARC records from a variety of sources whenever they can, and make their own records only when they cannot find records anywhere else.

- Patrons can search for bibliographic information in MARC records in much the same way that they used to search for that information on cards (browse searching). They can also tap the additional power of the computer to do keyword searching. The records that display in a computer catalog seldom look like catalog cards anymore, and often look quite different from catalog to catalog. However, regardless of how the computer records may display to patrons or staff, the bibliographic information and MARC coding in the records are the same (always assuming they are the same MARC records, of course).

- It is important to know the meaning of the terms used in this and other MARC-related documents. Staff who have to deal with MARC records will have to learn a few new terms, but should be pleased to find that many of the same cataloging terms that were used in the old catalog card days are still used in this new computer world.

- Catalogers and systems people will need to know MARC intimately. However, other library staff may be surprised at how much more comfortable they will feel about their library automation system if they know a bit more about the MARC fields that affect their various areas of endeavor.

- MARC coding is not that hard to learn if you understand the *why* of it.

Because MARC is *the* standard that we use in our libraries to facilitate sharing records and resources, we hope that we have been able to convince you that MARC is important to *you* and *your* library.

If you have read this far, it should also have struck you by now that MARC alone is not the end of the story. In fact, a MARC record in a library setting simply picks up where the cataloging rules leave off. The cataloging rules dictate what bibliographic information we will provide in our catalogs—MARC is simply our current method of coding that information into something that a computer can read.

Even so, because MARC is *the* currently accepted standard for providing bibliographic information in library catalogs, you have to understand that those standards are very precise and very detailed. They may be more detailed than some people would prefer, but, given time and your interest, we can assure you that a MARC expert could justify the usefulness of (just about) every code in the manual.

For example, before reading this book you might have questioned the usefulness of indicators. Now, however, you know that indicators are *very* important, because they tell the system something about the data in the fields in which they are found. Incorrect tracing indicators can prevent fields that should be indexed from being indexed. Incorrect filing indicators can file headings in places where they do not belong and where they (the headings) cannot be found. Incorrect display constant indicators can show confusing labels to patrons. Other indicators that are incorrect can do other undesirable things.

If you wondered about why we need subfields, you now know that they are very necessary to tell the system to "index this subfield in this index and that subfield in that index," or to "display these subfields, but not those." Without subfields we could not be so precise in our indexing instructions to the system, and so would lose some of the accuracy that we supply for searching.

If you were ignoring fixed-field data when making your records (000 and 008 in particular), you now know that you are depriving your patrons of useful qualifiers to allow them to narrow searches that would otherwise retrieve too many hits to be useful.

Given the precision required in coding a MARC record, we hope that we have at least been able to persuade you that "quality" is not just a worn-out word that you can ignore, especially in this age of automation. If the records in your MARC database are brief, incomplete, and/or riddled with cataloging and/or coding errors, then it does not matter how good your library automation system may be, or how much you paid for it, because access to your materials will be hampered by the poor quality of your MARC records.

We urge you to make the commitment to ensure that your database has good MARC records, and to at least learn enough about MARC to know whether your records have problems.

If nothing else, learning a bit about MARC will allow noncatalogers to communicate better with catalogers.

And if you are a cataloger, then you are in charge of making sure that your MARC records are good, so you need to take the time to *really* learn MARC *and* the cataloging rules. It will take time; there is much more to be learned than you will find in this introductory book. But there is no point in a cataloger saying that he or she cannot learn all the nitpicky cataloging details (no time, no support for training, no training available locally, it's just too hard!). Every cataloger *must* learn the details of cataloging, or we will never achieve our goal—to help patrons to find any material in any library anywhere in the world—and that *is* our goal, is it not?

12

MARC21 Sample Records

Here are five sample records to help you practice reading MARC21 bibliographic records.

Sample Record 1

```
LDR      00876cam 2200277 a 4500
001          00123456
003      DLC
008      001023t20001999jm a      db     001 0 eng
Entrd: 001023       DtSt: t  Dates: 2000, 1999    Ctry: jm  Ills: a
Audn:       Form: d  Cont: b  GPub:      Conf: 0   Fest: 0
Indx: 1   M/E:      LitF: 1  Biog:     Lang: eng  MRec:      Srce:
010      ‡a   00123456
020      ‡a0805205569
040      ‡aDLC‡cDLC‡dDLC
050      ‡aF1872‡b.F8
100 1    ‡aFoster, Deb.
245 10   ‡aJamaica mine‡h[text (large print)] :‡bcataloging on an
             island /‡cby Deb and Rick Foster.
246 30   ‡aCataloging on an island
250      ‡a1st ed.
260      ‡aKingston, Jamaica :‡bCHOC,‡c2000, c1999.
300      ‡a93 p. :‡bill. ;‡c24 cm. +‡e1 videocassette (60 min. :
             sd., col. ; 1/2 in.)
440  0   ‡aCaribbean culture series
490 1    ‡aIslands in the sun
504      ‡aIncludes bibliographical references and index.
651  0   ‡aJamaica‡xDescription and travel.
651  0   ‡aJamaica‡xSocial conditions.
650  0   ‡aCataloging‡zJamaica.
700 1    ‡aFoster, Rick.
710 2    ‡aCatalogers Helping Other Catalogers, Inc.
800 1    ‡aFoster, Deb.‡tIslands in the sun.
```

1. What are the personal name headings in this record?

    _____

2. Suppose we wanted to add another subject heading for Bob Marley. What tag would we use?

    _____

3. What tag and subfield contains the subtitle of this record?

    _____

4. Is the title in this record indexed?   Yes [   ]   No [   ]

Sample Record 2

```
000 00876cem  2200277 i 4500
001      97682807 /MAPS
003 DLC
008 970602s1995    bccabcg a    1    eng
Entrd: 970602    DtSt: s  Dates: 1995,      Ctry: bcc
Relf: abcg  Proj:              CrTp: a  GPub:   Indx: 1
SpFm:       Lang: eng  MRec:   Srce:
010     $a  97682807 /MAPS
020     $a0921463316
040     $aDLC$cDLC$dDLC
050 00 $aG4961.E635 1995$b.I8
110 2  $aITMB Publishing Ltd.
245 13 $aAn international travel map, Jamaica, scale 1:250,000.
246 1  $iAlternate title:$aJamaica
255    $aScale 1:250,000.
260    $aVancouver, B.C. :$bInternational Travel Maps,$cc1995.
300    $a1 map :$bcol. ;$c45 x 100 cm., folded to 23 x 15 cm.
500    $aRelief shown by contours, shading, gradient tints, and spot heights.
500    $aIncludes index, distance chart, location map, ancillary maps of Port
          Antonio, Ocho Rios, and Mandeville, text, and col. ill.
500    $aIndexed map of Kingston and maps of Montego Bay and Spanish Town on
          verso.
651 0 $aJamaica$vMaps, Tourist.
651 0 $aKingston (Jamaica)$vMaps.
710 2 $aInternational Travel Maps (Firm)
```

1. What character is being used as the subfield delimiter in this display?

_____

2. Is the title in this record indexed?

Yes [ ]   No [ ]

3. What does the second indicator in the 245 tell the system?

_____

4. What tag and subfield shows the date of publication to the patrons?

_____

5. According to the second indicator, where do both subject headings in this record come from?

_____

Sample Record 3

```
000 00876cam  2200277 a 4500
001    90070178 /AC
003 DLC
008 900208s1991    ilua    j be  001 0deng
Entrd: 900208 DtSt: s     Dates: 1991, Ctry: ilu      Ills: a
Audn: j  Form:    Cont: be GPub:  Conf: 0Fest: 0
Indx: 1  M/E:     Fict: 0  Biog: dLang: eng      Mrec:  Srce:
010     $a 90070178 /AC
020     $a0716601915
040     $aDLC$cDLC
050 00 $aAG6$b.C48 1991
082 00 $a031$220
245 00 $aChildcraft :$bthe how and why library.
246 3  $aChild craft.
260     $aChicago : World Book, Inc.,$cc1991.
300     $a15 v. :$bill. (some col.) ;$c26 cm.
504     $aIncludes bibliographical references and index.
520     $aIllustrated articles, stories, and poems, grouped thematically in
          fifteen volumes under titles including "World and space," "About
          animals," "How things work," and "Make and do."
655 7  $aChildren's encyclopedias and dictionaries.$21csh
650 1  $aEncyclopedias and dictionaries.
```

1. What field/subfield contains the LCCN?

_____

2. Does the system know that this record has publisher information?

   Yes [ ]   No [ ]

3. Is this title indexed?

   Yes [ ]   No [ ]

4. Will the 246 in this record display to patrons?

   Yes [ ]   No [ ]

Sample Record 4

```
000 00876njm  2200277 a 4500
001 qpq01000345
003 FM1bTMQ
008 700603c19671966oncrc                    eng
Entrd: 700603  DtSt: c  Dates: 1967,1966 Ctry: onc  Comp: rc
FMus:      Audn:        Form:        AccM:
LTxt:      Lang: eng    Mrec:        Srce:
010     $a   91750724
028 01 $aTN-3$bTrue North
040     $aDLC$cDLC
043     $an-cn---
090     $aTrue North WTN-3
100 1  $aCockburn, Bruce.
245 10 $aHigh winds white sky$h[sound recording] /$call selections written by
          Bruce Cockburn.
260     $a[Ontario?] :$bTrue North ;$aDon Mills, Ont. :$bDistributed by CBS
          Records Canada, $cp1971.
300     $a1 sound disc :$banalog, 33 1/3 rpm, stereo. ;$c12 in.
511 0  $aBruce Cockburn, vocals and guitar ; with other instrumentalists.
518     $aRecorded Nov. 1970-Apr. 1971, principally at Thunder Sound Studios,
          Toronto.
505 0  $aHappy good morning blues -- Let us go laughing -- Love song -- One day
          I walk -- Golden serpent blues -- High winds white sky -- You point to
          the sky -- Life's mistress -- Ting/The cauldron -- Shining mountain.
650  0 $aPopular music$zCanada$y1961-1970.
```

1. According to the leader, what type of record is this?

_____

2. If I searched "shining mountain" in the title keyword index, would I find this record?

   Yes [ ]   No [ ]

3. What will the display constant indicator (I1) of the 505 show to the patrons?

_____

Sample Record 5

```
000 01308ngm  2200349Ki 450Q
001 qpq93001267
003 FM1bTMQ
008 930707p19931992nyu110        vleng d
Entrd: 930707  DtSt: p  Dates: 1993,1992 Ctry: nyu  Time: 110
Audn:      AccM:         GPub:         Form:
TMat: v  Tech: l      Lang: eng   Mrec:         Srce: d
020    $a079281715X
245 00 $aOf mice and men$h[videorecording] /$cMetro-Goldwyn-Mayer presents a
       Russ Smith/Gary Sinise Production ; produced by Russ Smith and Gary
       Sinise ; directed by Gary Sinise.
260    $aCulver City, Calif. :$bMGM/UA Home Video,$cc1993.
300    $a1 videocassette (110 min.) :$bsd., col. ;$c1/2 in.
538    $aVHS Hi-fi
546    $aClosed captioned for the hearing impaired.
500    $aBased on the novel by John Steinbeck.
511 1  $aJohn Malkovich, Gary Sinise, Casey Siemaszko, Ray Walston,
       Sherilyn Fenn.
521 8  $aMPAA Rating : PG-13.
506    $aFor private home use only.
655  7 $aVideo recordings for the hearing impaired.$21csh
710 2  $aMetro-Goldwyn-Mayer.
700 1  $aMalkovich, John.
700 1  $aSinise, Gary.
700 1  $aSiemaszko, Casey.
700 1  $aWalston, Ray, 1917-
700 1  $aFenn, Sherilyn.
700 1  $aSteinbeck, John,$d1902-1968.$tOf mice and men.
```

1. According to the leader, what type of record is this?

_____

2. If I qualified a subject search for videos by "published in California," would I find this record?

   Yes [ ]   No [ ]

3. Which heading in this record is a corporate added entry?

_____

Quiz and Sample Records Answers

Quiz 1

1. Which particular needs of people are we addressing in this book?

    Educational, informational and recreational needs

2. How did people search our collections in the "very distant past" to find out whether we had materials that could meet those needs?

    By physically scanning our shelves of books and other items

3. How do patrons explore our collections now?

    By searching our catalogs to see descriptions of our materials

4. What do we call the information that patrons are supposed to use to decide whether our materials will meet their needs?

    Bibliographic information

5. What format do we use to code this information in computer records for our automated systems?

    The MARC format

Quiz 2

1. What are the six main "areas of information" that we provide for patrons when we describe material?

    a) Title and statement of responsibility
    b) Edition
    c) Publication details
    d) Physical description
    e) Series
    f) Notes

2. What are these "areas of information" called?

    Bibliographic descriptions

3. Why do we need to make our descriptions so detailed and accurate?

   So that patrons can tell from the computer screen whether we really have what they want

4. What four types of information do we provide so that patrons can search by them?

   a) Author (MARC field: 1XX)
   b) Title (MARC field: 130, 240, 245, 246)
   c) Series (MARC field: 440, 8XX)
   d) Added entries, such as editors, related authors, related titles, etc. (MARC field: 7XX)

5. What is this searchable information called?

   Access points or headings

6. What do we call the process of "establishing" headings and providing "cross-references"?

   Authority control

7. AACR2 tells us what bibliographic information to provide, then MARC tells us how to code that information for a computer record.

8. Why do we need all these rules and standards?

   So that we can be consistent in the bibliographic information that we provide in our MARC records.

Quiz 3

1. Where was MARC first developed?

   At the Library of Congress.

2. Are all machine-readable cataloging records MARC records?

   [   ] Yes   [x] No

   The term *MARC* stands for Machine Readable Cataloging, but not all machine-readable cataloging records are MARC records.

3. Is UNIMARC the same as MARC21?

   [   ] Yes   [x] No

   UNIMARC, IberMARC, NORMARC, and many other national MARCs are still not quite the same as MARC21.

4. Has MARC21 changed since it was first set up in the 1960s?

   [x] Yes   [   ] No

   That is another important point about MARC: it changes!

5. Do all the codes in a MARC21 bibliographic record have the same meaning in a MARC21 authority record?

   [   ] Yes   [x] No

   The coding in the different types of MARC21 records is similar in many ways, but there are enough differences to make the records very distinct. You can never assume that a code in a MARC21 bibliographic record will have the same meaning in a MARC21 authority record.

6. How do we get MARC21 bibliographic records?

   By making them ourselves or copying them from someone else.

Quiz 4

1. What does the abbreviation OPAC stand for?

    Online Public Access Catalog, aka WebPAC, the library's catalog on computer.

2. In an OPAC, what is a hitlist?

    An alphabetical list of "hits" or "matches" on a search.

3. What kind of search allows us to find any word anywhere in a heading or an indexed field in a MARC record?

    [ ] Browse   [x] Keyword

    Keyword searches find any word anywhere in a heading or an indexed field.

4. Do all OPAC displays look alike?

    [ ] Yes   [x] No

    Each system vendor may have different ideas about what patrons want to see, so not only will records in an Advance system, for example, display quite differently than records in a Voyager system, but also records in two Voyager systems can display quite differently, depending on how they are initially set up.

5. Do all MARC displays look the same?

    [ ] Yes   [x] No

    Unfortunately, each system can, and usually does, display MARC records differently.

Quiz 5

Connect the following terms to the MARC record

The leader   A tag   An indicator   Edition area   Statement of responsibility

```
000    00876cam  2200277 a 4500
001    00123456
003    DLC
008    001023t20001999jm a      db      001 0 eng
Entrd: 001023         DtSt: t  Dates: 2000, 1999      Ctry: jm  Ills: a
Audn:      Form: d   Cont: b   GPub:      Conf: 0   Fest: 0
Indx: 1   M/E:       LitF: 1   Biog:      Lang: eng  MRec:      Srce:
010    ‡a  00123456
020    ‡a0805205569
040    ‡aDLC‡cDLC‡dDLC
050    ‡aF1872‡b.F8
100 1  ‡aFoster, Deb.
245 10 ‡aJamaica mine‡h[text (large print)] :‡bcataloging on an
        island /‡cby Deb & Rick Foster
246 30 ‡aCataloging on an island
250    ‡a1st ed.
260    ‡aKingston, Jamaica :‡bCHOC,‡c2000, c1999.
300    ‡a93 p. :‡bill. ;‡c24 cm. +‡e1 videocassette (60 min :
        sd., col. ; 1/2 in.)
440  0 ‡aCaribbean culture series
490 1  ‡aIslands in the sun
504    ‡aIncludes bibliographical references and index.
651  0 ‡aJamaica‡xDescription and travel.
651  0 ‡aJamaica‡xSocial conditions.
650  0 ‡aCataloging‡zJamaica.
700 1  ‡aFoster, Rick.
710 2  ‡aCatalogers Helping Other Catalogers
800 1  ‡aFoster, Deb.‡tIslands in the sun.
```

A field   A note field   A subfield delimiter   A subfield code

Quiz 6

1. Which MARC fields will matter most to circulation, acquisitions, and ILL people?

   Number fields (which affect record matching) and display fields (which contain the description of an item).

2. Which MARC fields will matter most to reference people?

   Indexed fields (which affect how patrons can search) and display fields (which affect what patrons can see).

3 Which MARC fields will matter most to catalogers and systems people?

   All fields.

4. What is the least that directors should know about MARC?

   Garbage in, garbage out.

Quiz 7

1. What tag would I use for a:

   Personal name main entry? 100

   Corporate name added entry? 710

   Conference name subject? 611

   See figure 7-2, "Patterns in MARC Headings Tags"

2. If I search "Shakespeare" in a name browse index, will I find the following?

   ```
   600 10 $aShakespeare, William,$d1564-1616.
   ```

   [ ] Yes   [x] No

   The field is a 600 (a subject field), so even though the field contains a name, that name is indexed in the subject index, not the name index.

3. If I search "Unesco" in a subject browse index, will I find the following?

   ```
   610 20 $aUnesco.
   ```

   [x] Yes   [ ] No

   Field 610 is a subject field and is one of those indexed in the subject indexes.

4. If I search "Central Intelligence Agency" in a subject keyword index, will I find the following?

   ```
   610 20 $aUnited States.$bCentral Intelligence Agency$xHistory
   ```

   [x] Yes   [ ] No

   Field 610 is a subject field and is one of those indexed in the subject indexes. Because a keyword search will find any word anywhere in the field, it will find "Central Intelligence Agency," even though the term is not at the beginning of the field.

Quiz 8

1. If I search "Saint vs. Scotland Yard" in a title browse index, will I find the following?

```
100 1  $aCharteris, Leslie,$d1907-
245 04 $aThe Saint vs. Scotland Yard
```

[ ] Yes　　[x] No

Although 245 fields are indeed indexed in the title browse index, in this instance, the title is not the main entry. Leslie is, and because the title is not the main entry, it is not automatically indexed. The first indicator in the 245 is telling the system that it does not need to make a title added entry, so there won't be any entry for the title.

2. If I search "Saint vs. Scotland Yard" in a title browse index, will I find the following?

```
100 1  $aCharteris, Leslie,$d1907-
245 10 $aThe Saint vs. Scotland Yard
```

[ ] Yes　　[x] No

This time, although the first indicator is saying to make an added entry for the title, the second indicator is telling the system to start indexing at the "T" in "The" instead of at the proper place, the "S" in "Saint."

3. If I search "Utopian adventure" in a title browse index, will I find the following?

```
245 10 $aSpending :$ba utopian divertimento /$cMary Gordon.
246 02 $aA utopian adventure
```

[ ] Yes　　[x] No

Although 246 fields are indeed indexed in the title browse index, in this case, although the second indicator is correctly telling the system to start indexing at "U" rather than "A," the first indicator is telling the system to display the field, but not index it.

4. If I search "Copeland studies" in a title browse index, will I find the following?

```
100 1  $aTebeau, Charlton W.
245 10 $aMan in the Everglades.
440  0 $aCopeland studies in Florida history ;$vno. 3
```

[x] Yes　　[ ] No

Because 440 fields are indexed in title browse, and the second indicator is correctly coded to start the indexing at the "C" in Copeland, this example is correct.

5. If I search "chronicles of Narnia" in a title browse index, will I find the following?

```
100 1  $aLewis, C. S. $q(Clive Staples),$d1898-1963.
245 10 $aThe Lion, the witch and the wardrobe.
490 0  $aThe chronicles of Narnia
```

[ ] Yes　　[x] No

Because 490 fields are not indexed in the title browse index, this example is incorrect.

Quiz 9

1. If I qualify a search by type of material = sound recording, will I find the following?

```
000      00876nam  2200277 a 4500 (Type of record = "a")
245 00 $aSound of music soundtrack$h[sound recording].
300     $a1 sound cassette :$banalog
```

[ ] Yes   [x] No

The leader/type of record is coded "a," which is telling the system that the record is for language material, e.g., a book. That code should be either "i" (nonmusical sound recording) or "j" (musical sound recording), as appropriate.

2. If I qualify a search by date = 1998, will I find the following?

```
008  Date 1: 1998
260     $aNew York :$bBantam,$c1999.
```

[x] Yes   [ ] No

The 008 date 1 is telling the system that the item was published in 1998, even though the 260$c is telling the patrons that it was published in 1999.

3. If I qualify a search by language = Spanish, will I find the following?

```
008  Lang: eng
245 04 $aLos muros de agua.
```

[ ] Yes   [x] No

Even though the title looks Spanish, the 008 language code eng is telling the system that the item is in English.

5. How many 008s can there be in a MARC record?

One, and there *must* be one.

Quiz 10

1. Must a MARC record have an 001 field?

[x] Yes   [ ] No

The 001 is a mandatory field.

2. Do 010 fields have indicators?

[x] Yes   [ ] No

They are both blank and have no meaning.

3. Are number fields important for patrons?

[x] Yes   [ ] No

Number fields can be useful for searching.

4. Are number fields important for library automation systems?

[x] Yes   [ ] No

Number fields are useful for machine matching records to prevent duplicate records from showing up in the OPAC, but they can cause bad matches to occur, so great care must be taken with these matching fields.

Sample Record 1

```
LDR      00876cam 2200277 a 4500
001         00123456
003     DLC
008     001023t20001999jm a       db      001 0 eng
Entrd:  001023      DtSt: t  Dates: 2000, 1999    Ctry: jm  Ills: a
Audn:       Form: d  Cont: b  GPub:      Conf: 0   Fest: 0
Indx: 1  M/E:      LitF: 1  Biog:      Lang: eng  MRec:      Srce:
010     ‡a  00123456
020     ‡a0805205569
040     ‡aDLC‡cDLC‡dDLC
050     ‡aF1872‡b.F8
100 1   ‡aFoster, Deb.
245 10  ‡aJamaica mine‡h[text (large print)] :‡bcataloging on an
           island /‡cby Deb and Rick Foster.
246 30  ‡aCataloging on an island
250     ‡a1st ed.
260     ‡aKingston, Jamaica :‡bCHOC,‡c2000, c1999.
300     ‡a93 p. :‡bill. ;‡c24 cm. +‡e1 videocassette (60 min. :
           sd., col. ; 1/2 in.)
440  0  ‡aCaribbean culture series
490 1   ‡aIslands in the sun
504     ‡aIncludes bibliographical references and index.
651  0  ‡aJamaica‡xDescription and travel.
651  0  ‡aJamaica‡xSocial conditions.
650  0  ‡aCataloging‡zJamaica.
700 1   ‡aFoster, Rick.
710 2   ‡aCatalogers Helping Other Catalogers, Inc.
800 1   ‡aFoster, Deb.‡tIslands in the sun.
```

1. What are the personal name headings in this record?

   100—Foster, Deb. and 700—Foster, Rick. (800—Foster, Deb. Islands in the sun. is actually a personal name series added entry—a name/title heading to pick up the title.)

2. Suppose we wanted to add another subject heading for Bob Marley. What tag would we use?

   600 10 ‡aMarley, Bob.

3. What tag and subfield contains the subtitle of this record?

   245‡b

4. Is the title in this record indexed?

   [x] Yes   [ ] No

   The first indicator of the 245 says to make a title added entry, because the 245 is not the main entry—Foster, Deb is.

Sample Record 2

```
000 00876cem 2200277 i 4500
001     97682807 /MAPS
003 DLC
008 970602s1995    bccabcg a     1     eng
Entrd: 970602        DtSt: s  Dates: 1995,        Ctry: bcc
Relf: abcg  Proj:            CrTp: a   GPub:    Indx: 1
SpFm:        Lang: eng   MRec:   Srce:
010     $a  97682807 /MAPS
020     $a0921463316
040     $aDLC$cDLC$dDLC
050 00  $aG4961.E635 1995$b.I8
110 2   $aITMB Publishing Ltd.
245 13  $aAn international travel map, Jamaica, scale 1:250,000.
246 1   $iAlternate title:$aJamaica
255     $aScale 1:250,000.
260     $aVancouver, B.C. :$bInternational Travel Maps,$cc1995.
300     $a1 map :$bcol. ;$c45 x 100 cm., folded to 23 x 15 cm.
500     $aRelief shown by contours, shading, gradient tints, and spot heights.
500     $aIncludes index, distance chart, location map, ancillary maps of Port
          Antonio, Ocho Rios, and Mandeville, text, and col. ill.
500     $aIndexed map of Kingston and maps of Montego Bay and Spanish Town on
          verso.
651 0   $aJamaica$vMaps, Tourist.
651 0   $aKingston (Jamaica)$vMaps.
710 2   $aInternational Travel Maps (Firm)
```

1. What character is being used as the subfield delimiter in this display?

    The dollar sign $.

2. Is the title in this record indexed?

    [x] Yes   [   ] No

    See question 4 under sample record 1.

3. What does the second indicator in the 245 tell the system?

    To skip three characters before beginning to index, i.e., to begin indexing at the "i" in "international," not the "A" in "An."

4. What tag and subfield shows the date of publication to the patrons?

    260$c

5. According to the second indicator, where do both subject headings in this record come from?

    I2 = 0, so the subject headings come from LCSH.

Sample Record 3

```
000 00876cam  2200277 a 4500
001    90070178 /AC
003 DLC
008 900208s1991    ilua    j be   001 0deng
Entrd: 900208  DtSt: s     Dates: 1991,  Ctry: ilu      Ills: a
Audn: j  Form:    Cont: be GPub:  Conf: 0Fest: 0
Indx: 1  M/E:     Fict: 0  Biog: dLang: eng     Mrec:  Srce:
010    $a 90070178 /AC
020    $a0716601915
040    $aDLC$cDLC
050 00 $aAG6$b.C48 1991
082 00 $a031$220
245 00 $aChildcraft :$bthe how and why library.
246 3  $aChild craft.
260    $aChicago : World Book, Inc.,$cc1991.
300    $a15 v. :$bill. (some col.) ;$c26 cm.
504    $aIncludes bibliographical references and index.
520    $aIllustrated articles, stories, and poems, grouped thematically in
          fifteen volumes under titles including "World and space," "About
          animals," "How things work," and "Make and do."
655 7  $aChildren's encyclopedias and dictionaries.$2lcsh
650 1  $aEncyclopedias and dictionaries.
```

1. What field/subfield contains the LCCN?

    010

2. Does the system know that this record has publisher information?

    [ ] Yes   [x] No

    The patron can see "World Book, Inc." and figure out that it is the publisher, but because there is no $b to tell the system that it is a publisher, the system thinks it is part of the place of publication $a.

3. Is this title indexed?

    [x] Yes   [ ] No

    Even though the second indicator of the 245 is telling the system not to index the title as an added entry, because the title is the main entry (since there is no 1XX field to be the main entry), it is automatically indexed.

4. Will the 246 in this record display to patrons?

    [ ] Yes   [x] No

    The first indicator is 3, which means "do not display, but index."

Sample Record 4

```
000  00876njm  2200277 a 4500
001  qpq01000345
003  FM1bTMQ
008  700603c19671966oncrc               eng
Entrd: 700603  DtSt: c   Dates: 1967,1966 Ctry: oncComp: rc
FMus:       Audn:       Form:       AccM:
LTxt:       Lang: eng   Mrec:       Srce:
010     $a 91750724
028 01  $aTN-3$bTrue North
040     $aDLC$cDLC
043     $an-cn---
090     $aTrue North WTN-3
100 1   $aCockburn, Bruce.
245 10  $aHigh winds white sky$h[sound recording] /$call selections written by
          Bruce Cockburn.
260     $a[Ontario?] :$bTrue North ;$aDon Mills, Ont. :$bDistributed by CBS
          Records Canada, $cp1971.
300     $a1 sound disc :$banalog, 33 1/3 rpm, stereo. ;$c12 in.
511 0   $aBruce Cockburn, vocals and guitar ; with other instrumentalists.
518     $aRecorded Nov. 1970-Apr. 1971, principally at Thunder Sound Studios,
          Toronto.
505 0   $aHappy good morning blues -- Let us go laughing -- Love song -- One day
          I walk -- Golden serpent blues -- High winds white sky -- You point to
          the sky -- Life's mistress -- Ting/The cauldron -- Shining mountain.
650  0  $aPopular music$zCanada$y1961-1970.
```

1. According to the leader, what type of record is this?

    A musical sound recording, code j.

2. If I searched "shining mountain" in the title keyword index, would I find this record?

    [x] Yes   [ ] No

    Field 505 is indexed in title keyword, and "Shining mountain" is one of the song titles listed in the 505.

3. What will the display constant indicator (I1) of the 505 show to the patrons?

    Contents:

Sample Record 5

```
000 01308ngm  2200349Ki 450Q
001 qpq93001267
003 FM1bTMQ
008 930707p19931992nyu110          vleng d
Entrd: 930707  DtSt: p  Dates: 1993,1992 Ctry: nyu  Time: 110
Audn:         AccM:        GPub:        Form:
TMat: v   Tech: 1        Lang: eng    Mrec:         Srce: d
020    $a079281715X
245 00 $aOf mice and men$h[videorecording] /$cMetro-Goldwyn-Mayer presents a
          Russ Smith/Gary Sinise Production ; produced by Russ Smith and Gary
          Sinise ; directed by Gary Sinise.
260    $aCulver City, Calif. :$bMGM/UA Home Video,$cc1993.
300    $a1 videocassette (110 min.) :$bsd., col. ;$c1/2 in.
538    $aVHS Hi-fi
546    $aClosed captioned for the hearing impaired.
500    $aBased on the novel by John Steinbeck.
511 1  $aJohn Malkovich, Gary Sinise, Casey Siemaszko, Ray Walston,
          Sherilyn Fenn.
521 8  $aMPAA Rating : PG-13.
506    $aFor private home use only.
655  7 $aVideo recordings for the hearing impaired.$21csh
710 2  $aMetro-Goldwyn-Mayer.
700 1  $aMalkovich, John.
700 1  $aSinise, Gary.
700 1  $aSiemaszko, Casey.
700 1  $aWalston, Ray, 1917-
700 1  $aFenn, Sherilyn.
700 1  $aSteinbeck, John,$d1902-1968.$tOf mice and men.
```

1. According to the leader, what type of record is this?

    Projected medium, code g.

2. If I qualified a subject search for videos by "published in California," would I find this record?

    [ ] Yes   [x] No

    The country code in the 008 is nyu, which is New York.

3. Which heading in this record is a corporate added entry?

    710 Metro-Goldwyn-Mayer.

MARC21 Bibliographic Code List

(as of Feb. 2002)

TAG	DESCRIPTION
000	LEADER
001	CONTROL NUMBER
003	CONTROL NUMBER IDENTIFIER
005	DATE AND TIME OF LATEST TRANSACTION
006	FIXED-LENGTH DATA ELEMENTS—ADDITIONAL MATERIAL CHARACTERISTICS
007	PHYSICAL DESCRIPTION FIXED FIELD
008	FIXED-LENGTH DATA ELEMENTS
010	LIBRARY OF CONGRESS CONTROL NUMBER
013	PATENT CONTROL INFORMATION
015	NATIONAL BIBLIOGRAPHY NUMBER
016	NATIONAL BIBLIOGRAPHIC AGENCY CONTROL NUMBER
017	COPYRIGHT REGISTRATION NUMBER
018	COPYRIGHT ARTICLE—FEE CODE
020	INTERNATIONAL STANDARD BOOK NUMBER
022	INTERNATIONAL STANDARD SERIAL NUMBER
024	OTHER STANDARD IDENTIFIER
025	OVERSEAS ACQUISITION NUMBER
027	STANDARD TECHNICAL REPORT NUMBER
028	PUBLISHER NUMBER

TAG	DESCRIPTION
030	CODEN DESIGNATION
032	POSTAL REGISTRATION NUMBER
033	DATE/TIME AND PLACE OF AN EVENT
034	CODED CARTOGRAPHIC MATHEMATICAL DATA
035	SYSTEM CONTROL NUMBER
036	ORIGINAL STUDY NUMBER FOR COMPUTER DATA FILES
037	SOURCE OF ACQUISITION
039	LEVEL OF BIBLIOGRAPHIC CONTROL AND CODING DETAIL
040	CATALOGING SOURCE
041	LANGUAGE CODE
042	AUTHENTICATION CODE
043	GEOGRAPHIC AREA CODE
044	COUNTRY OF PUBLISHING/PRODUCING ENTITY CODE
045	TIME PERIOD OF CONTENT
046	SPECIAL CODED DATES
047	FORM OF MUSICAL COMPOSITION CODE
048	NUMBER OF MUSICAL INSTRUMENTS OR VOICES CODE
050	LIBRARY OF CONGRESS CALL NUMBER
051	LIBRARY OF CONGRESS COPY, ISSUE, OFFPRINT STATEMENT
052	GEOGRAPHIC CLASSIFICATION
055	CALL NUMBERS/CLASS NUMBERS ASSIGNED IN CANADA
060	NATIONAL LIBRARY OF MEDICINE CALL NUMBER
061	NATIONAL LIBRARY OF MEDICINE COPY STATEMENT
066	CHARACTER SETS PRESENT
070	NATIONAL AGRICULTURAL LIBRARY CALL NUMBER
071	NATIONAL AGRICULTURAL LIBRARY COPY STATEMENT
072	SUBJECT CATEGORY CODE
074	GPO ITEM NUMBER
080	UNIVERSAL DECIMAL CLASSIFICATION NUMBER
082	DEWEY DECIMAL CALL NUMBER
084	OTHER CLASSIFICATION NUMBER
086	GOVERNMENT DOCUMENT CLASSIFICATION NUMBER
088	REPORT NUMBER
100	MAIN ENTRY—PERSONAL NAME
110	MAIN ENTRY—CORPORATE NAME

TAG	DESCRIPTION
111	MAIN ENTRY—MEETING NAME
130	MAIN ENTRY—UNIFORM TITLE
210	ABBREVIATED TITLE
211	ACRONYM OR SHORTENED TITLE
212	VARIANT ACCESS TITLE
214	AUGMENTED TITLE
222	KEY TITLE
240	UNIFORM TITLE
242	TRANSLATION OF TITLE BY CATALOGING AGENCY
243	COLLECTIVE UNIFORM TITLE
245	TITLE STATEMENT
246	VARYING FORM OF TITLE
247	FORMER TITLE OR TITLE VARIATIONS
250	EDITION STATEMENT
254	MUSICAL PRESENTATION STATEMENT
255	CARTOGRAPHIC MATHEMATICAL DATA
256	COMPUTER FILE CHARACTERISTICS
257	COUNTRY OF PRODUCING ENTITY FOR ARCHIVAL FILMS
260	PUBLICATION, DISTRIBUTION, ETC. [IMPRINT]
261	IMPRINT STATEMENT FOR FILMS (pre-AACR2)
262	IMPRINT STATEMENT FOR SOUND RECORDINGS (pre-AACR2)
263	PROJECTED PUBLICATION DATE
265	SOURCE FOR ACQUISITION/SUBSCRIPTION ADDRESS
270	ADDRESS
300	PHYSICAL DESCRIPTION
306	PLAYING TIME
307	HOURS, ETC.
310	CURRENT PUBLICATION FREQUENCY
321	FORMER PUBLICATION FREQUENCY
340	PHYSICAL MEDIUM
342	GEOSPATIAL REFERENCE DATA [PROVISIONAL]
343	PLANAR COORDINATE DATA [PROVISIONAL]
351	ORGANIZATION AND ARRANGEMENT OF MATERIALS
352	DIGITAL GRAPHIC REPRESENTATION [PROVISIONAL]
355	SECURITY CLASSIFICATION CONTROL

TAG	DESCRIPTION
357	ORIGINATOR DISSEMINATION CONTROL
362	DATES OF PUBLICATION AND/OR SEQUENTIAL DESIGNATION
400	SERIES STATEMENT/ADDED ENTRY—PERSONAL NAME
410	SERIES STATEMENT/ADDED ENTRY—CORPORATE NAME
411	SERIES STATEMENT/ADDED ENTRY—MEETING NAME
440	SERIES STATEMENT/ADDED ENTRY—TITLE
490	SERIES STATEMENT
500	GENERAL NOTE
501	WITH NOTE
502	DISSERTATION NOTE
504	BIBLIOGRAPHY, ETC. NOTE
505	FORMATTED CONTENTS NOTE
506	RESTRICTIONS ON ACCESS NOTE
507	SCALE NOTE FOR GRAPHIC MATERIAL
508	CREATION/PRODUCTION CREDITS NOTE
510	CITATION/REFERENCES NOTE
511	PARTICIPANT OR PERFORMER NOTE
513	TYPE OF REPORT AND PERIOD COVERED NOTE
514	DATA QUALITY NOTE
515	NUMBERING PECULIARITIES NOTE
516	TYPE OF COMPUTER FILE OR DATA NOTE
518	DATE/TIME AND PLACE OF AN EVENT NOTE
520	SUMMARY, ETC.
521	TARGET AUDIENCE NOTE
522	GEOGRAPHIC COVERAGE NOTE
524	PREFERRED CITATION OF DESCRIBED MATERIALS NOTE
525	SUPPLEMENT NOTE
526	STUDY PROGRAM INFORMATION NOTE
530	ADDITIONAL PHYSICAL FORM AVAILABLE NOTE
533	REPRODUCTION NOTE
534	ORIGINAL VERSION NOTE
535	LOCATION OF ORIGINALS/DUPLICATES NOTE
536	FUNDING INFORMATION NOTE
538	SYSTEM DETAILS NOTE
540	TERMS GOVERNING USE AND REPRODUCTION NOTE

TAG	DESCRIPTION
541	IMMEDIATE SOURCE OF ACQUISITION NOTE
544	LOCATION OF OTHER ARCHIVAL MATERIALS NOTE
545	BIOGRAPHICAL OR HISTORICAL DATA
546	LANGUAGE NOTE
547	FORMER TITLE COMPLEXITY NOTE
550	ISSUING BODY NOTE
552	ENTITY AND ATTRIBUTE INFORMATION NOTE
555	CUMULATIVE INDEX/FINDING AIDS NOTE
556	INFORMATION ABOUT DOCUMENTATION NOTE
561	OWNERSHIP AND CUSTODIAL HISTORY
562	COPY AND VERSION IDENTIFICATION NOTE
565	CASE FILE CHARACTERISTICS NOTE
567	METHODOLOGY NOTE
580	LINKING ENTRY COMPLEXITY NOTE
581	PUBLICATIONS ABOUT DESCRIBED MATERIALS NOTE
583	ACTION NOTE
584	ACCUMULATION AND FREQUENCY OF USE NOTE
585	EXHIBITIONS NOTE
586	AWARDS NOTE
600	SUBJECT ADDED ENTRY—PERSONAL NAME
610	SUBJECT ADDED ENTRY—CORPORATE NAME
611	SUBJECT ADDED ENTRY—MEETING NAME
630	SUBJECT ADDED ENTRY—UNIFORM TITLE
650	SUBJECT ADDED ENTRY—TOPICAL TERM
651	SUBJECT ADDED ENTRY—GEOGRAPHIC NAME
653	INDEX TERM—UNCONTROLLED
654	SUBJECT ADDED ENTRY—FACETED TOPICAL TERMS
655	INDEX TERM—GENRE/FORM/PHYSICAL CHARACTERISTICS
656	INDEX TERM—OCCUPATION
657	INDEX TERM—FUNCTION
658	INDEX TERM—CURRICULUM OBJECTIVE
700	ADDED ENTRY—PERSONAL NAME
710	ADDED ENTRY—CORPORATE NAME
711	ADDED ENTRY—MEETING NAME
720	ADDED ENTRY—UNCONTROLLED NAME

TAG	DESCRIPTION
730	ADDED ENTRY—UNIFORM TITLE
740	ADDED ENTRY—UNCONTROLLED RELATED/ANALYTICAL TITLE
752	ADDED ENTRY—HIERARCHICAL PLACE NAME
753	SYSTEM DETAILS ACCESS TO COMPUTER FILES
754	ADDED ENTRY—TAXONOMIC IDENTIFICATION
755	ADDED ENTRY—PHYSICAL CHARACTERISTICS
760	MAIN SERIES ENTRY
762	SUBSERIES ENTRY
765	ORIGINAL LANGUAGE ENTRY
767	TRANSLATION ENTRY
770	SUPPLEMENT/SPECIAL ISSUE ENTRY
772	PARENT RECORD ENTRY
773	HOST ITEM ENTRY
774	CONSTITUENT UNIT ENTRY
775	OTHER EDITION ENTRY
776	ADDITIONAL PHYSICAL FORM ENTRY
777	ISSUED WITH ENTRY
780	PRECEDING ENTRY
785	SUCCEEDING ENTRY
786	DATA SOURCE ENTRY
787	NONSPECIFIC RELATIONSHIP ENTRY
800	SERIES ADDED ENTRY—PERSONAL NAME
810	SERIES ADDED ENTRY—CORPORATE NAME
811	SERIES ADDED ENTRY—MEETING NAME
830	SERIES ADDED ENTRY—UNIFORM TITLE
840	SERIES ADDED ENTRY—TITLE
841	HOLDINGS CODED DATA VALUES
842	TEXTUAL PHYSICAL FORM DESIGNATOR
844	NAME OF UNIT
843	REPRODUCTION NOTE
845	TERMS GOVERNING USE AND REPRODUCTION NOTE
850	HOLDING INSTITUTION
851	LOCATION
852	LOCATION
853	CAPTIONS AND PATTERN—BASIC BIBLIOGRAPHIC UNIT

TAG	DESCRIPTION
854	CAPTIONS AND PATTERN—SUPPLEMENTARY MATERIAL
855	CAPTIONS AND PATTERN—INDEXES
856	ELECTRONIC LOCATION AND ACCESS
863	ENUMERATION AND CHRONOLOGY—BASIC BIBLIOGRAPHIC UNIT
864	ENUMERATION AND CHRONOLOGY—SUPPLEMENTARY MATERIAL
865	ENUMERATION AND CHRONOLOGY—INDEXES
866	TEXTUAL HOLDINGS—BASIC BIBLIOGRAPHIC UNIT
867	TEXTUAL HOLDINGS—SUPPLEMENTARY MATERIAL
868	TEXTUAL HOLDINGS—INDEXES
870	VARIANT PERSONAL NAME
871	VARIANT CORPORATE NAME
872	VARIANT CONFERENCE OR MEETING NAME
873	VARIANT UNIFORM TITLE HEADING
876	ITEM INFORMATION—BASIC BIBLIOGRAPHIC UNIT
877	ITEM INFORMATION—SUPPLEMENTARY MATERIAL
878	ITEM INFORMATION—INDEXES
880	ALTERNATE GRAPHIC REPRESENTATION
886	FOREIGN MARC INFORMATION FIELD
900	EQUIVALENCE AND CROSS-REFERENCE—PERSONAL NAME
910	EQUIVALENCE AND CROSS-REFERENCE—CORPORATE NAME
911	EQUIVALENCE AND CROSS-REFERENCE—CONFERENCE OR MEETING NAME
930	EQUIVALENCE AND CROSS-REFERENCE—UNIFORM TITLE HEADING
980	EQUIVALENCE AND CROSS-REFERENCE—SERIES STATEMENT—PERSONAL NAME/TITLE
981	EQUIVALENCE AND CROSS-REFERENCE—SERIES STATEMENT—CORPORATE NAME/TITLE
982	EQUIVALENCE AND CROSS-REFERENCE—SERIES STATEMENT—CONFERENCE OR MEETING NAME
983	EQUIVALENCE AND CROSS-REFERENCE—SERIES STATEMENT—TITLE/UNIFORM TITLE
990	LINK TO EQUIVALENCES OR CROSS-REFERENCES

APPENDIX
C

List of Initial Articles

CODE	LANGUAGE
a	English, Gallegan, Hungarian, Portuguese, Romanian, Scots, Yiddish
a'	Gaelic
al	Romanian
al-	Arabic, Baluchi, Brahui, Panjabi (Perso-Arabic script), Persian, Turkish, Urdu (*Note:* al- is meant to cover alternate romanizations of the initial article, e.g., *as-sijill*)
am	Gaelic
an	English, Gaelic, Irish, Scots, Yiddish
an t-	Gaelic, Irish
ane	Scots
ang	Tagalog
ang mga	Tagalog
as	Gallegan, Portuguese
az	Hungarian
bat	Basque
bir	Turkish
d'	English
da	Shetland English
das	German
de	Danish, Dutch, English, Friesian, Norwegian, Swedish
dei	Norwegian
dem	German
den	Danish, German, Norwegian, Swedish

CODE	LANGUAGE
der	German, Yiddish
des	German
det	Danish, Norwegian, Swedish
di	Yiddish
die	Afrikaans, German, Yiddish
dos	Yiddish
e	Norwegian
'e	Friesian
een	Dutch
eene	Dutch
egy	Hungarian
ei	Norwegian
ein	German, Norwegian
eine	German
einem	German
einen	German
einer	German
eines	German
eit	Norwegian
el	Catalan, Spanish
el-	Arabic
els	Catalan
en	Catalan, Danish, Norwegian, Swedish
et	Danish, Norwegian
ett	Swedish
eyn	Yiddish
eyne	Yiddish
ga	Tagalog
gl'	Italian
gli	Italian
ha-	Hebrew
hai	Classical Greek, Greek
he	Hawaiian
he	Classical Greek, Greek
he-	Hebrew
heis	Greek
hen	Greek
hena	Greek
henas	Greek
het	Dutch
hi	Icelandic
hin	Icelandic

CODE	LANGUAGE
hina	Icelandic
hinar	Icelandic
hinir	Icelandic
hinn	Icelandic
hinna	Icelandic
hinnar	Icelandic
hinni	Icelandic
hins	Icelandic
hinu	Icelandic
hinum	Icelandic
ho	Classical Greek, Greek
ho-	Hebrew
hoi	Classical Greek, Greek
i	Italian
ih'	Provençal
il	Italian, Provençal/Langue d'oc
il-	Maltese
in	Friesian
it	Friesian
ka	Hawaiian
ke	Hawaiian
l'	Catalan, French, Italian, Provençal/Langue d'oc
l-	Maltese
la	Catalan, Esperanto, French, Italian, Provençal/Langue d'oc, Spanish
las	Provençal/Langue d'oc, Spanish
le	French, Italian, Provençal/Langue d'oc
les	Catalan, French, Provençal/Langue d'oc
lh	Provençal/Langue d'oc
lhi	Provençal/Langue d'oc
li	Provençal/Langue d'oc
lis	Provençal/Langue d'oc
lo	Italian, Provençal/Langue d'oc, Spanish
los	Provençal/Langue d'oc, Spanish
lou	Provençal/Langue d'oc
lu	Provençal/Langue d'oc
mga	Tagalog
mia	Greek
'n	Afrikaans, Dutch, Friesian
na	Gaelic, Hawaiian, Irish
na h-	Gaelic, Irish
ny	Malagasy
'o	Neapolitan

CODE	LANGUAGE
o	Gallegan, Hawaiian, Portuguese, Romanian
os	Portuguese
'r	Icelandic
's	German
sa	Tagalog
sa mga	Tagalog
si	Tagalog
siná	Tagalog
't	Dutch, Friesian
ta	Classical Greek, Greek
tais	Classical Greek
tas	Classical Greek
te	Classical Greek
ten	Classical Greek, Greek
tes	Classical Greek, Greek
the	English
to	Classical Greek, Greek
tois	Classical Greek
ton	Classical Greek, Greek
tou	Classical Greek, Greek
um	Portuguese
uma	Portuguese
un	Catalan, French, Italian, Provençal/Langue d'oc, Romanian, Spanish
un'	Italian
una	Catalan, Italian, Provençal/Langue d'oc, Spanish
une	French
unei	Romanian
unha	Gallegan
uno	Italian, Provençal/Langue d'oc
uns	Provençal/Langue d'oc
unui	Romanian
us	Provençal/Langue d'oc
y	Welsh
ye	English
yr	Welsh

BIBLIOGRAPHY

All works cited within the text appear here, along with a few background documents.

Anglo-American Cataloguing Rules (AACR). 1998. 2nd ed., 1998 rev. Chicago: American Library Association.

Crawford, Walt. 1989. *MARC for Library Use.* 2nd ed. Boston: G. K. Hall.

Cutter, Charles Ammi. 1904. *Rules for a Dictionary Catalog.* 4th ed., rewritten. Washington, D.C.: G.P.O.

Dewey, Melvil. 1996. *Dewey Decimal Classification and Relative Index.* 21st ed. 4 vols. Albany, N.Y.: Forest Press.

Fritz, Deborah A. 1999. *Cataloging with AACR2R and USMARC.* Chicago: American Library Association.

Gorman, Michael. 2001. *From Card Catalogues to WebPACS.* Final version. Online document. 5 December 2001. http://www.loc.gov/catdir/bibcontrol/Gorman_paper.html.

Hildreth, Charles R. 1995. "Stages in the Development of Online Catalogs." In *Online Catalog Design Models: Are We Moving in the Right Direction?* Online document. 3 December 2001. http://phoenix.liunet.edu/~hildreth/clr-two.html.

Initial Definite and Indefinite Articles. 2000. Online document. 7 January 2002. http://lcweb.loc.gov/marc/bibliographic/bdapp-e.html.

International Federation of Library Associations and Institutions (IFLA). 2000. *Functional Requirements for Bibliographic Records—Final Report.* Online document. 3 December 2001. http://www.ifla.org/VII/s13/frbr/frbr1.htm.

LC Classification Schedules. Multiple vols. Irregular. Washington, D.C.: Library of Congress.

Library of Congress Subject Headings. Annual. Washington, D.C.: Library of Congress.

MARC Code List for Organizations. 2000. Online document. 5 January 2002. http://lcweb.loc.gov/marc/organizations/.

MARC21 Concise Format for Bibliographic Data. 1999. English ed., update no. 1, October 2000. Online document. 5 December 2001. http://lcweb.loc.gov/marc/bibliographic/ecbdhome.html.

MARC Development. 2001. Online document. 7 January 2002. http://lcweb.loc.gov/marc/development.html.

MARC Forum. 2001. Website. 7 December 2001. http://lcweb.loc.gov/marc/marcformum.html.

MARC Standards. 2001. Website. 7 January 2002. http://lcweb.loc.gov/marc/.

OCLC. *Bibliographic Formats and Standards.* 1993. Online document. 7 January 2002. http://www.oclc.org/oclc/bib/about.htm.

Sears, Minnie Earl. 1997. *Sears List of Subject Headings.* 15th ed. New York: Wilson.

Subject Cataloging Manual: Subject Headings. 2000. Washington, D.C.: Library of Congress.

Understanding MARC Bibliographic. 2000. 5th ed. Online document. 7 January 2002. http://lcweb.loc.gov/marc/umb.

GLOSSARY

Definitions not original to this glossary have been adapted from:

Anglo-American Cataloguing Rules (AACR). 1998. 2nd ed., 1998 rev. Chicago: American Library Association.

Library Automation/Technology Glossary. Online document. 29 January 2002. http://www.library.hq.com/glossary.html.

ODLIS: Online Dictionary of Library and Information Science (ODLIS). Online document, 29 January 2002. http://vax.wcsu.edu/library/odlis.html.

Consult these or other similar sources for definitions of terms not listed in this glossary.

AACR2 *Anglo-American Cataloguing Rules,* 2nd ed., rev. The current nationally accepted cataloging rules for the United States, Great Britain, Canada, Australia, and most other English-speaking countries. (Not for the fainthearted.)

AC Headings *See* Annotated Card Program Subject Headings

access point A heading (e.g., name, title, or subject), keyword, code, or number (e.g., ISBN) by which a bibliographic record may be searched.

add item The process of searching one's own database of preexisting bibliographic records, finding a record that matches an item (according to match criteria standards), and adding local holdings information to the record.

added entry An access point in a bibliographic record, that is not the primary heading (main entry), but is considered important as a search term for a work. For example: joint authors, editors, illustrators, variant titles.

Annotated Card Program Subject Headings A list of subject headings that are specifically designed for use by children. Developed by the Library of Congress and included as a section in LCSH.

areas of information Specific parts of the bibliographic description of an item that are identified as important by the cataloging rules.

authority control The function of providing established headings as access points in bibliographic records and linking those headings to authority records that display, with appropriate cross references, in an OPAC.

authority record A computer record that contains an established heading for a name, title, or subject. The record may also contain links from variant forms of the heading (*see* references), links to other established headings (*see also* references), and notes about the heading.

authority work The process of deciding which name, title, or subject and which form of that name, title, or subject will be made the established heading for someone or something, for the sake of consistency in a library catalog. Also, the practice of providing appropriate cross references from unused headings to an established heading (*see* references) and to other established headings (*see also* references).

bad match The result of two records that represent different items being merged because one of the number fields used for machine matching is the same in both records.

barcode label A printed label that can be read by a barcode scanner. In a library, barcodes provide numbers that uniquely identify individual physical items in the library collection for circulation and inventory purposes, as well as individual patrons for circulation purposes.

bibliographic control The process of creating, organizing, and maintaining standardized bibliographic records that describe library materials, and providing access to those records so that library patrons might find, identify, select, and obtain access to those materials.

bibliographic description Descriptive data (specified by cataloging rules) provided in a bibliographic record to identify a particular edition of a work (e.g., title, edition, publication details, physical description details, and notes). From this description someone should be able to decide whether or not the materials represented by the description will meet his or her needs.

bibliographic information The bibliographic description and access points for an item.

bibliographic record A computer record that contains bibliographic information about a specific edition of a work.

bibliographic utility An organization that provides access to bibliographic and authority records, usually in MARC format, for the purpose of cooperative cataloging, interlibrary loan, and other related services.

brief record An OPAC display of minimal bibliographic information about an item—usually author, title, publisher, and physical description information. Holdings information (primarily the location, call number, and circulation status of the item) is also often shown in this brief display.

browse searching In a card catalog, flipping through cards organized alphabetically by their name, title, or subject headings. In an OPAC, entering the first word(s) of a heading in an appropriate index (usually name, title, or subject) to find records that contain headings that begin with the word(s). Sometimes called *exact searching.* Most useful when you know a name, title, or subject heading, or at least the beginning words of such information.

call number A sequence of numbers and letters assigned according to a given classification system and printed on a label attached to an item in a library collection. The item is shelved sequentially by the call number on its label. The call number is also provided in the bibliographic record for the item, making it possible for a patron to identify the item's location on the shelf.

Canadian Committee on MARC (CCM) A committee that makes recommendations to the National Library of Canada about changes to be made to the MARC21 format.

Canadian Subject Headings (CSH) A list of descriptive words or phrases specifically related to Canada that can be used as established headings to indicate the subject of a work. Developed by the National Library of Canada.

CANMARC format The specific MARC format developed and maintained by the National Library of Canada. Slightly different from MARC21 standards, it was brought into line with USMARC standards to form MARC21 in 1998.

card catalog Bibliographic information provided on three-by-five-inch cards that are filed alphabetically by headings typed at the tops of the cards.

catalog record *See* bibliographic record

cataloger Someone responsible for following cataloging rules to create bibliographic records for the items obtained by a library.

cataloging rules Standardized rules for providing bibliographic descriptions and access points for the cataloging of library materials. (Followed by some, ignored by others.)

Children's Headings *See* Annotated Card Program Subject Headings

classification system A method of grouping similar library materials together in an organized fashion to facilitate access to those materials.

coded field *See* control field

computer catalog *See* OPAC

computer record A record that can be read and processed by a computer.

control field In a MARC record, a field that contains coded information. The term is sometimes used to mean both the leader and the 008 combined.

controlled vocabulary A list of established headings that can be used to describe the subject of a work. May include cross-references to the established headings from variant or related headings.

cooperative cataloging An arrangement among a group of catalogers to share cataloging records. The first cataloger in the group to catalog an item follows standard cataloging rules (usually AACR) and coding standards (usually MARC) to create a bibliographic record in the union catalog. Other catalogers in the group are then able to copy that bibliographic record instead of having to do original cataloging to create their own record.

copy cataloging The process of searching an outside source of preexisting bibliographic records, finding a record that matches an item (according to match criteria standards), downloading that record (rather than having to make one from scratch), doing (it is hoped) minimal editing to improve the record, and adding local holdings information to the record.

corporate body "An organization or group of persons that is identified by a particular name and that acts, or may act, as an entity. Typical examples of corporate bodies are associations, institutions, business firms, nonprofit enterprises, governments, government agencies, religious bodies, local churches, and conferences" (AACR 1998, glossary, p. 617).

cross-reference A link that takes a searcher from an unused heading to a used heading (*see* references) or from a used heading to another related used heading (*see also* references).

database A collection of computer records.

deduping-on-the-fly The process of duplicate record detection performed when records from various databases are accessed via a search on a virtual union catalog. The objective is that only one bibliographic record for an item will be displayed to a searcher, with multiple libraries attached, rather than individual bibliographic records being displayed for each library that holds the same item.

Dewey Decimal Classification (DDC) A numeric classification system developed by Melvil Dewey that arranges library materials into broad subject classes indicated by numbers, with further subject subdivisions indicated by decimal numbers. Used primarily by public and school libraries.

dictionary catalog A card catalog in which headings are interfiled in a single alphabetic sequence, instead of being separated by types of headings, e.g., names, titles, and subjects. *See also* divided catalog

directory The long set of numbers that follows a leader in a MARC record. Seen only when the record is displayed in its raw communications format. These numbers tell a library automation system which fields are present in a MARC record, where each field begins, and how many characters each field contains.

display constant Text that is not present in a bibliographic record, but is displayed by a library automation system. In a MARC record, display constants are usually triggered by an indicator value (e.g., special labels for notes).

display field A field in a MARC record that contains descriptive information that is meant to be displayed to patrons in a library's OPAC. Some display fields are also indexed (e.g., 245—Title information; 440—Series title information). Other display fields are not usually indexed (e.g., 260—Publication information; 300—Physical description information).

divided catalog A card catalog in which headings are filed in separate alphabetic sequences for each type of heading: names, titles, or subjects. Most online catalogs have separate indexes for these different types of entries and so function like divided catalogs.

downloading records Transferring records from one computer to another.

duplicate record detection A machine process of comparing multiple records to determine whether those records are (essentially) the same.

element of an area A cataloging term for "a word, phrase, or group of characters representing a distinct unit of bibliographic information and forming part of an area . . . of the description" (AACR 1998, glossary, p. 617). Now synonymous with a MARC subfield.

established heading The official form of a name, title, series title, or subject that will be used consistently as a heading in bibliographic records in a library catalog.

exact searching *See* browse searching

extent of item The number of physical units and the SMD (specific material designation) of an item, e.g., "1 videocassette." For books of only one volume, the number of pages, leaves, etc., of the volume.

festschrift A collection of works written in honor of a person or scholarly society.

field A particular area in a record in which the same type of information is always entered. A collection of fields is called a *record*. In a MARC record: the entire string of information identified by a tag.

filing indicator An indicator value that is meant to tell a library automation system how many characters of an initial article to skip before beginning to index a title.

fixed field *See* control field

fixed-length field A field that is restricted to a specific number of characters. In a MARC bibliographic record used to refer to the 008 field.

form subdivision A subject subdivision that specifies the form of the material being described, e.g., when a work is a periodical or juvenile film.

format A clearly defined set of standards for arranging data in a computer record.

full record An OPAC display showing the complete bibliographic information about an item.

genre/form heading An established heading from a controlled vocabulary that expresses the theme (e.g., mystery, science fiction, western) or form (e.g., novel, short story) of a work.

GMD (General Material Designation) "A term indicating the broad class of material to which an item belongs (e.g., sound recording)" (AACR 1998, glossary, p. 618).

Guidelines on Subject Access to Individual Works of Fiction, Drama, Etc. (gsafd) A compilation of descriptive words or phrases that can be used as established headings to indicate the genre or form of a work. Developed by the American Library Association's Subject Analysis Committee.

heading A name, word, or phrase by which a bibliographic record may be searched. On a catalog card these names, words, or phrases are placed at the top of the card to indicate that the card is to be filed by them. In a computer catalog, headings are indexed in separate name, title, or subject indexes and are available for browse searching and keyword searching.

hitlist A list of all the results that match a search term.

hold If an item is not available because it is checked out by someone or is on-order (and so not yet in the library collection), a patron can put a hold on that item. When the item becomes available, the library will notify the patron.

holdings information Information about individual items in a library collection, including, but not limited to, the call number, the number from the barcode label attached to the item, the volume number if appropriate, and circulation status.

holdings record A record that contains holdings information.

importing records The process of loading records from an outside computer to your own library automation system. *See also* downloading records, duplicate record detection, machine matching.

imprint The statement on an item that identifies its publisher and its place and date of publication.

index An ordered list of access points. In an OPAC, specific types of indexes can be searched for specific categories of information, e.g., names, titles, subjects, numbers.

indexed field Not all fields in MARC records are indexed. Indexed fields are those that have been selected to be made searchable in an OPAC through browse and keyword searching.

indicator *See* indicator value

indicator position The first two character positions at the beginning of each variable-length field in a MARC record. The meaning of each indicator position is different (i.e., do not look at both positions together; consider them separately).

indicator value In a MARC record: a one-character code in an indicator position. The indicator value gives a library automation system special instructions about the data found in the field that follows.

initial article A word or words at the beginning of a title or a name, such as "The," "An," "A," "Los," "Las," or "Les." These words are meant to be ignored in indexing, unless they are a part of a proper name, e.g., "El Cid," "Las Vegas."

interlibrary loan (ILL) The process whereby an item that is found in the catalog of one library is loaned to the patron of another library.

invalid coding Coding used incorrectly in a MARC record. For example, a character used as a subfield code in a field where that character has not been defined as valid by the MARC standards.

ISBD punctuation Punctuation rules specified by AACR, taken from the International Standard Bibliographic Description rules for punctuation. Intended to help patrons and library staff to identify distinct elements of the bibliographic description of an item.

ISBN International Standard Book Number. A number assigned by a publisher to a specific edition of a work. It is supposed to be unique to that edition only (i.e., the first edition should have a different ISBN than the second edition), but it is often not unique.

item Library material in any physical format that can be treated as a single entity or thing and so can be assigned a single bibliographic description.

keyword A word found anywhere in an indexed field in a computer record.

keyword searching In an OPAC: entering word(s) on a search screen (usually name, title, subject, or general) to have the computer look for the word(s) anywhere in an indexed field. Most useful when you do not know the beginning words of an established heading (*see* browse searching), but remember a relevant word or phrase.

LCCN Library of Congress Control Number. Formerly typed at the bottom right of a catalog card (when it was called a Library of Congress Card Number). Now entered in the 010 field of a MARC record. Intended to apply only to the particular edition of a work that is described by the bibliographic record in the LC database. Publishers have been known to erroneously provide the LCCN for a previous edition in a later edition of a work.

LCMARC format *See* MARC21 format

LCSH *See* Library of Congress Subject Headings

leader The first twenty-four characters of a MARC record. The leader contains important information about the record itself, rather than about the item that the record is describing.

library automation system Computer software that automates some or all of the functions of a library, typically acquisitions, serials check-in, cataloging, and a public catalog (OPAC).

library catalog A compilation of bibliographic records that represent the materials in a specific library.

library consortium A nonprofit organization established to facilitate resource sharing and other shared activities among a group of libraries.

library network Organizations that act as regional brokers for bibliographic utilities.

Library of Congress (LC) The (unwilling) de facto national library of the United States of America. The largest single producer of MARC records. The entity to which libraries of all types look for guidance on interpreting the cataloging rules.

Library of Congress Classification (LCC) An alphanumeric classification system developed by the Library of Congress that arranges library materials into broad subject classes indicated by letters, with further subject subdivisions indicated by decimal numbers. Used primarily by academic and special libraries.

Library of Congress Subject Headings (LCSH) A compilation of descriptive words or phrases that can be used to indicate the subject of a work. Developed by the Library of Congress and used by all types of libraries.

limit searching *See* search limits

linking *See* add item

machine matching The machine process of comparing one bibliographic record to another bibliographic record and performing duplicate record detection to see if the records are the same. Often done when batch-loading records.

Machine-Readable Bibliographic Information Committee (MARBI) A committee of the American Library Association that makes recommendations to the Library of Congress about changes to be made to the MARC21 format.

main entry The primary access point for a bibliographic record. Can be a person or body solely or primarily responsible for the intellectual and/or artistic content of the work described by the record, or can be the title of the work.

MARC Machine Readable Cataloging Record. A standard for coding bibliographic information into a computer record.

MARC communications format *See* MARC format

MARC display A display in an OPAC that shows bibliographic records or authority records in MARC tagged format.

MARC format A generic term for a variety of similar but slightly different types of standards, initially developed by LC, that provide a method of organizing bibliographic data for communication and storage, e.g., MARC21 format, UKMARC format.

MARC record Technically, any computer record structured to follow the MARC format. In the context of this book, the phrase usually refers to a bibliographic record in the MARC21 format.

MARC standards *See* MARC format

MARC21 authority record An authority record coded for a computer, using the specific standards dictated by the MARC21 format to make authority control possible in a library catalog.

MARC21 bibliographic record A bibliographic record coded for a computer, using the specific standards dictated by the MARC21 format to provide bibliographic information.

MARC21 format The specific MARC format developed by the Library of Congress and maintained by LC and the National Library of Canada. Slightly different from UKMARC and other MARC formats.

MARC21 holdings record A holdings record coded for a computer, using the specific standards dictated by the MARC21 format to provide holdings information.

MARC21 standards *See* MARC21 format

match criteria A set of conditions that must be met in order to match an item with a bibliographic record. Currently, OCLC's criteria, as found in its *Bibliographic Formats and Standards* manual, are the most widely disseminated standards available for matching.

Medical Subject Headings (MeSH) A compilation of descriptive words or phrases specifically related to medicine that can be used as established headings to indicate the subject of a work. Developed by the National Library of Medicine.

MicroLIF Microcomputer Library Interchange Format. A standard for coding bibliographic records, developed by library automation system vendors in the mid-1980s for data transfer via diskettes. Based on, but not exactly the same as, the MARC21 format. Brought into line with MARC21 in 1991 as MicroLIF91.

MicroLIF91 A standard for coding bibliographic records, developed by library automation system vendors for data transfer via diskettes. MicroLIF is not consistent with MARC21 standards for coding, but MicroLIF91 is.

monograph A cataloging term for "an item either complete in one part or complete, or intended to be completed, in a finite number of separate parts" (AACR 1998, glossary, p. 620).

name/title added entry An added entry that consists of both the name of a person or corporate body responsible for a work and the title of the work (in which case, the added entry is really for the work, not the person or body).

National Union Catalog (NUC) 754 volumes (print or microfiche) published between 1968 and 1981. Each volume includes hundreds of photocopies of printed catalog cards from LC and other research libraries. These cards are arranged alphabetically by title, many to a page, and need a magnifying lens to be read. Used for copy cataloging and interlibrary loan purposes. Continued, in effect, by the OCLC online union catalog.

number field A field in a MARC record that contains a number that is usually searchable in an OPAC through a special index or keyword searching. Some examples of number fields are 010 (LCCN), 020 (ISBN), 050 (LC call number), 082 (Dewey call number).

obsolete coding Coding in a MARC record that was once defined by the MARC standards to have a specific meaning, but now is no longer supposed to be used.

OCLC An international bibliographic utility originating in the United States in Dublin, Ohio. As of this writing, its database contains over 50 million bibliographic records and authority records in MARC21 format. Member libraries use this database and special software to do cooperative cataloging, interlibrary loans, and other related services.

online catalog *See* OPAC

on-order A term meaning that an item has been ordered from a publisher or other source, but has not yet been received by a library. Some libraries put bibliographic records in their catalogs for on-order items, to let patrons and staff know that they will soon be available.

OPAC Online Public Access Catalog. A library catalog made up of bibliographic records in machine-readable format (usually MARC format) available via computer.

original cataloging The process of creating a bibliographic record for an item from scratch.

outsourcing In a cataloging context: paying someone else to do your cataloging for you.

PAC *See* OPAC

parallel title The title proper of an item in a different language or script.

patron record A record that contains information about a library member for use in the circulation module of a library automation system. No MARC standard currently exists for coding this information.

qualify searching *See* search limits

record A set of information about an entity, usually composed of separate fields that each describe a separate aspect of the entity. For example, a bibliographic record contains bibliographic information about an item.

repeatable In a MARC record: whether or not a given field can be entered more than once in a record, or a given subfield can be entered more than once in a field. For example, field 100 is not repeatable, so you can enter only one 100 field in a MARC record, but field 246 is repeatable, so you can enter as many 246 fields in a record as you wish. In a 245 field, subfield $a is not repeatable, so you can enter only one subfield $a in a 245 field, but subfield $p is repeatable, so you can enter as many subfield $p's in a 245 field as you need.

resource sharing A variety of activities resulting from formal or informal agreements between libraries to share materials. Often used synonymously with *interlibrary loan.*

RLG Research Libraries Group. A member-based organization made up of over sixty large universities, archives, museums, etc., that maintains a union catalog called RLIN. This database contains many millions of bibliographic records and authority records in MARC21 format. Member libraries use this database and special software to do cooperative cataloging, interlibrary loans, and other related services.

RLIN Research Libraries Information Network. An international bibliographic utility originating in the United States, primarily used by research and large academic libraries. Member libraries use this database and a special interface to do cooperative cataloging, interlibrary loans and other related services.

search limits In an OPAC: an option on a search screen that allows a user to reduce the number of hits retrieved by a search term. The most commonly found search limits are date of publication, language, and type of material.

search screen A display screen in an OPAC on which the user can select a particular index and enter a search term.

Sears List of Subject Headings A compilation of descriptive words or phrases that can be used as established headings to indicate the subject of a work. Developed by Minnie E. Sears and first published in 1923. Narrower in scope and with more general subject headings than LCSH. Used by small public or school libraries.

see also **reference** A link from an established heading that is used in a library catalog to another related established heading that is also used in the same catalog. *See also* cross-reference

see **reference** A link from a form of heading or entry that is not used in a library catalog to the established heading that is used. *See also* cross reference

serial A publication issued in successive parts and intended to be issued indefinitely, including magazines, newspapers, journals, yearbooks, etc.

series A group of separately published items with unique titles that are connected to one another by the presence of another title that is common to each item.

series, traced A series title that is to be indexed exactly as it is shown on an item.

series, untraced or traced differently A series title that either is not to be indexed at all (untraced) or is to be indexed differently than it is shown on an item (traced differently).

shared database A database of bibliographic records to which the holdings information of multiple libraries is attached.

shared system A library automation system jointly shared by a group of libraries. May have a shared database and shared patron records, or may have those files kept separate.

shelflist catalog A card catalog, arranged in call number order, for the use of library staff. Primarily used for inventory purposes.

SMD (Specific Material Designation) The most specific designation provided by the cataloging rules to say what an item is. For example, the SMD for an audiocassette is "sound cassette."

statement of responsibility A statement in a bibliographic record that follows the title of a work and indicates the person(s) or corporate body or bodies responsible for the intellectual or artistic content of the work. This statement is usually copied exactly as it is given on the chief source of information of the work.

subfield A discrete portion of a field in which the same type of information is always entered. Fields are broken down into subfields when data elements in a field require separate manipulation. In a MARC record: the contents of a subfield are identified by the subfield code.

subfield code A single, lowercase, alphanumeric character that follows a subfield delimiter and precedes data elements within a field. Subfield codes define what the contents of a subfield will be.

subfield delimiter A single character (ASCII 031) to tell a computer program that the character following is a subfield code, not part of the subfield information. May be displayed differently in different library automation systems, but often shown as a double dagger (‡) or dollar sign ($).

Subject Cataloging Manual Guidelines for assigning subject headings and subject subdivisions in a consistent and standardized manner.

subject heading An established heading from a controlled vocabulary that expresses one topic or theme of a work.

subject subdivision A word or phrase added to a subject heading to make it more specific in meaning.

subordinate body "A corporate body that forms an integral part of a larger body in relation to which it holds an inferior hierarchical rank" (AACR 1998, glossary, p. 623).

subsequent title When individual titles for different works are listed on a chief source of information, a subsequent title is any title after the first title.

subtitle Wording found after a title proper that explains, expands upon, or limits the meaning of the title.

tag In a MARC record: the three-digit label for a field that identifies its contents.

title page A page at the beginning of a book where one can find the title proper of the item, and usually the author or other persons or corporate bodies responsible for the work.

thesaurus A list of subject terms that provides a specialized vocabulary for a particular area of interest. Used to assign subject headings in bibliographic records.

title proper The primary name of an item, usually found on the chief source of information for the item, e.g., a title page of a book.

tracing indicator An indicator value that is meant to tell a library automation system whether or not to index a field. Comes from the fact that tracings were typed as headings on separate cards so they could be searched.

tracings At the bottom of a catalog card: the list of all the headings typed on other cards and filed in the catalog for that work. In a MARC context: indexed fields.

UKMARC format The specific MARC format developed and maintained by the British Library. Slightly different from MARC21 standards.

uniform title A cataloging term for "the particular title by which a work that has appeared under varying titles is to be identified for cataloging purposes" (AACR 1998, glossary, p. 624).

union catalog A library catalog of the materials held in more than one library. Created by loading the records from the databases of multiple libraries into one single database. This database can then be searched to show which libraries hold which materials.

union database *See* union catalog

Universal Decimal Classification (UDC) A numeric classification system based on DDC that adds symbols to numbers to allow greater flexibility in arranging library materials into broad subject classes. Used primarily by special libraries.

USMARC format *See* MARC21 format

Utlas Originally the University of Toronto Library Automation System, it spun off to become the bibliographic utility for Canada; now defunct.

variable-length field A field that is not restricted to any specified length. The maximum length of a variable-length field in a MARC record is 9,999 characters.

variable-length record A record that is not restricted to any specific length. MARC records are variable-length records. The maximum length of a MARC record is 99,999 characters.

variant title A variation of the title proper of an item, e.g., a title found on the spine or cover of a book that is slightly different from the title on the title page.

virtual union catalog A library catalog of the materials held in more than one library. Created by linking the databases of member libraries online, so that they can be searched simultaneously to show which libraries hold which materials.

WebPAC An OPAC that is accessed using a web browser

work A distinct intellectual or artistic creation, per the IFLA *Functional Requirements for Bibliographic Records* (FRBR).

Z39.50 protocol A standard established by the National Information Standards Organization (NISO) that allows a user of one Z39.50-compliant library automation system to search a different Z39.50-compliant library automation system.

INDEX

Deborah A. Fritz is the co-owner of The MARC of Quality, a Florida-based company that provides training, software, and database services to help librarians create better MARC records. Formerly a cataloging trainer at a multitype library consortium and a cataloger at various libraries, she currently teaches an extensive array of cataloging workshops around the United States. She is the author of *Cataloging with AACR2 and USMARC: For Books, Computer Files, Serials, Sound Recordings, and Videorecordings* (ALA, 1999). She is co-developer of several MARC processing programs, including *MARC Report* and *MARC Global.* Fritz earned her master's degree in library science at the University of Toronto.

Richard Fritz is the other half of The MARC of Quality. Formerly a library systems administrator for a medium-sized school district and, before that, in charge of authority control cleanup at a large bibliographic utility, his professional career has always involved MARC database processing in some capacity. His current work includes designing MARC processing software *MARC Report* and *MARC Global* for use by the library community and for in-house processing. He earned his library degree at the University of Toronto and also holds two other master's degrees.